Telling Jews about Jesus

Telling Jews about Jesus

Paul Morris

Grace Publications

GRACE PUBLICATIONS
139 Grosvenor Avenue
London N5 2NH
England

Managing Editors
J.P. Arthur, M.A.
H.J. Appleby

ISBN 0 946462 32 1

Distributed by
EVANGELICAL PRESS
12 Wooler Street
Darlington
Co. Durham DL1 1RQ
England

Cover design by Mike Moore

Printed in Great Britain by The Bath Press, Avon

Contents

Preface

Shalom and welcome! In this book you are entering, in a small way, into the world of the Jews. It is my aim to encourage and equip you to witness to your Jewish friends. The Jewish world is a fascinating one, filled with interesting people and dramatic events, but it is a mundane one as well, containing much that is routine and humdrum. It is also one with much suffering and heartache. Above all, it is a world which God began and with which He is still intimately involved, a world from which Jesus Christ came and the Christian Church emerged, a world to which you as a Christian are intimately connected, as firmly as a branch is to a tree.

You are probably reading this book because you have a Jewish friend and want some advice on how to witness about Jesus as the Saviour. Perhaps you feel that you do not have time to study the Jews and Judaism in detail, but nevertheless want some help. This book is designed for you. It may be encouraging to know that among all the Jewish people who believe in Jesus, most of them gained their first interest through the testimony of a Christian friend, someone like you.

Introduction

Facing our fears

No doubt you do not like to be rejected; you are a normal human being and you like to be well thought of! Perhaps you have experienced this fear of rejection rising quickly when you have realised that the person to whom you want to witness is Jewish; perhaps you have become tongue-tied. Somehow you sense that it is a part of a Jewish person's make-up and culture to reject Jesus as Messiah, and you are just not sure how to put things in a relevant and sensitive way. On top of that you may feel that he or she knows the Bible well, which makes you a bit cautious. Some of the following chapters are designed to give you an understanding of the Jewish people and of Jewish thinking, with its many different shades, and this will help you to understand your Jewish friend better. God alone can take away our fear of man, but understanding is very important for removing our feelings of uncertainty.

Becoming like a Jew

The Apostle Paul did not have to read a book to learn about the Jewish or the Gentile world, he was brought up in both. You probably do not have that advantage, and so you have to put in a bit more effort! This book will help you, but it is also important to have a listening ear. I was greatly helped in understanding the Jews by visiting a simple but pious old Jewish woman every week for several

years and just listening to all she had to say of her past in Hungary
and her experiences in this country. By listening I learnt what her
day-to-day Judaism and Jewish life-style were and what they meant
to her. I am not saying that you will have to wait years before you
can really understand, or before you should speak of Jesus, but
simply that you should ask questions in an indirect and conversa-
tional manner, and then listen. This also means that you are treating
your friend as an individual, not as 'a Jew'; you will soon find that
Jewish people can be very varied.

To gain this understanding and sensitivity is a major step towards
becoming 'like a Jew' when you witness to a Jewish friend. In
practice it means you will be prepared to alter the way you express
the Gospel to him. If you study the way Paul preached the Gospel
to the Jews in the synagogue at Antioch (Acts 13v13-48) and how
he preached it to Gentiles on Mars Hill (Acts 17v16-34) you will see
the difference. In the former Paul announced a promise fulfilled, in
the latter he spoke of ignorance overlooked. Becoming like a Jew
also means you will be prepared to alter your behaviour to a degree,
as Paul describes how he did in 1 Corinthians 9v19-23. This does not
mean you try to become a Jew by growing a beard (if you are a man!)
and eating only kosher food. Your Jewish friend will not respect you
for that; he will see it as a 'put-on'. But when you are with him it will
mean, as far as is possible, observing his conventions and following
his lifestyle. To become like a Jew means you continue to be
yourself, but with that sensitivity to your Jewish friend which makes
you willing to adapt to his preferences.

Remembering God's power

It does not all depend on you. Hopefully you know that already! As
you have read the Acts of the Apostles you have no doubt rejoiced
at all those people believing in the Lord Jesus. How wonderful to
preach a sermon and see 3,000 people saved! Has it ever struck you
that they were all Jews, religious Jews, some of whom had travelled
hundreds of miles to be in Jerusalem at Pentecost? Such people are
not today's idea of prime candidates for conversion. As time went
on thousands more Jews believed, in the land of Israel and in other
parts of the Roman Empire. The Church began as a powerful work
of God among the people to whom He had promised the Messiah,

giving them the task of going out to tell the Gentiles. God has already done great things among the Jews. "Is anything too hard for the LORD?" He can save your Jewish friend too.

1.
Being a Christian

This chapter should be a reminder of something you already know: what you say is judged against the background of what you are. If your manner and lifestyle are not consistent with the message you proclaim you have swept the ground from under your own feet. There is a sense in which you must be the message.

When Jesus called men to work with Him in the task of making disciples He did not begin by telling them the ABC of the message, followed by a course in communication skills. He began with the words 'follow me'. When the Apostles were brought before the Sanhedrin it was not their learning and quickness of reply which impressed those men, in fact they 'perceived that they were uneducated and untrained men'. They were impressed with their boldness and took note of the fact that 'they had been with Jesus'. There is a world of truth here and it must be emphasised right at the start. Christlikeness is a vital component in communicating the message of Christ. All that is said in this book assumes that this is understood and that you are seeking to live a consistent Christian life. No insight I can give, or method that I can suggest will make up for a lack in that area.

Consistent Christian living is important for your witness to anyone but it is especially so with Jewish people because they have an understandably negative view of Christians and Christianity. In their history they are more conscious of experiencing intolerance and persecution at the hands of professing Christians than love and kindness. A Christian who shows love and is willing to admit his faults can neutralise a great deal of a Jewish person's cultural reaction against the Gospel. This was frequently demonstrated in the middle of last century when many Jews fled from eastern Europe because of persecution by professing Christians. You would think that they would have been put off Christianity for life, but in fact significant numbers were saved. This was because in many of the places to which they fled they saw true Christianity and heard the true Gospel.

Of course this point should not be stretched too far. God does save people despite the most ungracious and inconsistent Christian messengers. Nothing can limit His power to save, and it seems that at times He delights to allow as many obstacles in the way as possible so as to show His sovereign power. However we cannot presume on the mysteries of His ways, as Moses said, 'The secret things belong to the LORD our God but those things which are revealed belong to us...'(Deuteronomy 29v29). Our part is to follow what He has shown, so that by the things we do and the way we speak, Jews are attracted to Jesus.

All this is not meant to make you freeze with fear, or to give you the impression that you can only speak about the Lord after ten years of growing as a Christian. Consistent Christianity is not perfection, rather it is the experience of righteousness, peace, and joy in the Holy Spirit, coupled with a humble desire to improve. Where your Jewish friend sees sincerity in these things he will be drawn to what you say. This is true of all types of Jews, whether the irreligious or the more forbidding – looking orthodox. All are spoken to by a changed human life, by a life which exemplifies what they would like to be. Never underestimate a lifestyle which is 'worthy of the Gospel of Christ', and never overestimate the value of a multitude of words in the absence of Christian love.

2.
Jews are just as human!

If someone comes from a culture different from ours we may be inclined to see him as a different sort of human being! If a highly qualified foreigner is interviewed on a documentary programme, there is a tendency for some from Western cultures to have doubts about what he says, especially if they already disagree with him, simply because he is from the Third World. This stems partly from arrogance, and partly from the difficulty we all find in looking past the superficial differences to the central similarities. This problem can arise in witnessing to a Jewish friend. You may already know he is Jewish, or you may discover it in the course of a conversation, and your natural reaction is to erect a mental barrier between him and yourself. All you know or do not know about Jews makes you apprehensive and throws you off balance. This is understandable, but there are two ways in which it can be conquered: firstly by remembering that the humanity you share with a Jewish person is more significant than the religious and cultural differences that separate you, and secondly by coming to understand those religious and cultural differences. In subsequent chapters I will deal with the latter, but in this one I want to deal with the significance of our common humanity. One Jewish wit put it like this, 'We Jews are the same as everyone else, only more so!'

Jews are spiritually the same

Lost
Jewish people are not only the seed of Abraham, they are the seed

of Adam, and when Paul says 'in Adam all die' he includes his own people. As human beings, Jews come under the same universal condemnation that God passed upon the whole human race when Adam fell. They, like others, stand hopelessly guilty before God. Because of this they too are born with a fallen human nature and are under the dominion of their sinful desires. They too are under the wrath of God. When we look at Jewish friends we look at those who are, as we were, guilty and condemned, living sinfully and unable to change themselves or to truly love God. They are heading for everlasting punishment. If that does not move us to pity and compassion nothing else will.

Mistaken

When people are faced with the fact of their sin their instinctive human reaction is 'Yes, but…' They imagine that there is something about them or their circumstances which makes them an exception. This too is sin. It is simply copying Adam, who blamed God after he had sinned because God had given him Eve in the first place! Instead of owning up we bury the truth deep and then, out of a hat so to speak, produce some amazing excuse for ourselves. We all do this in our own way, and the Jewish way is a very convincing one because they seem to have God on their side.

I am referring to the Jewish attitude to the law given at Sinai. God gave them that law, so He must think they are able to keep it. He must be generally pleased with them. This is where the majority of the Jews were and are mistaken. Many have used the fact that God gave them the law as an excuse for not taking it too seriously. Paul put it like this 'for not the hearers of the law are just in the sight of God, but the doers of the law will be justified… you call yourself a Jew and you rely on the law… you then who teach others, do you not teach yourself?' Elsewhere Paul makes it plain why the law was given, 'Whatever the law says, it says to those who are under the law, that every mouth may be stopped and all the world may become guilty before God… for by the law is the knowledge of sin.' It was given so as to paint sin in bolder colours and so drive the Jewish people to God for mercy. They, however, buried this awareness and made the great mistake of thinking that possessing and hearing the law was enough.

Because of this, righteousness with God became simply a matter of doing their best to keep the law, as Paul writes, 'but Israel, pursuing the law of righteousness, has not attained to the law of righteousness. Why? Because they did not seek it by faith, but as it were, by the works of the law.' In this the Jews are just like the good moral people you often meet who are convinced God will be satisfied with their having done their best. The difference is that the Jews see themselves as privileged to have received God's law so as to guide them more certainly in His will. They assume God is confident they can do it. It is a great mistake!

Of course, not all Jews are concerned to keep the law in all its details, but it has deeply affected Jewish thinking. Therefore even when an irreligious Jew is pressed about his failures he will rest in the fact that somehow being Jewish helps; on top of which he does his best, and is not as bad as a few others he could mention. What you have to do is to show your Jewish friend that the law was not given as a ladder to heaven, but rather to show him his sin and so drive him to God for his salvation.

None of this is meant to belittle the fact that God gave the law as a covenant code for Israel to obey. It was to be taken seriously by all Israelites as the way of living which was pleasing to God. The mistake was to see such obedience as their justification.

Called

'Where are you?' were God's first words to Adam after he had sinned, and He has been calling men back to Himself ever since. The Jews have a unique place in this activity of God because He created them as a special people through whom He would give His written truth to the world. Through the spread of that truth He calls all men back to Himself; but it was to Israel that the truth was first given — to call them to repentance and faith. God gave them the written law, and continually raised up prophets to teach Israel, and at times to call them back. Finally He sent His Son.

Jesus' call was summarised by Mark in these words 'Repent and believe the gospel'. The apostles took up that plea to Israel with 'Repent and let everyone of you be baptised in the name of Jesus Christ for the remission of sins.' It is the same call today. Jewish people have no hope of salvation without faith in Jesus the Messiah. He alone has made the atoning sacrifice necessary for sins to be forgiven. Israel's whole history is one of God calling them to

Himself through the law and the Gospel. Today He is still calling them to Himself, by those of us who have believed.

Whatever differences of culture and religious background may mark you out from your Jewish friend this much you have in common spiritually: he is lost as you were, he is mistaken as you were, and God is calling him like you to trust His Son.

Jews are naturally the same

The Jews do not live on an outpost of planet Earth! They live on it with you and me and therefore they share its common experiences. We often allow differences of culture to obscure this, but Jews are looking for a contented and purposeful life in this world like everyone else. In that quest they will experience fulfilment and frustration, attainments and disappointments, joys and also griefs. This gives you a point of contact with a Jewish friend. Such experiences come your way too, but you know God in your life leading and assuring you, and when there seems no answer to your question 'Why?' you can trust that He knows best. As you discuss or share in life's experiences with a Jewish person you can be sure that your testimony of God in your life will be very relevant to him.

In fact it is dangerous to draw too hard a line between the natural and the spiritual. Is it not true that one of God's ways of calling us back to Himself is to frustrate us in our quest for an easy and contented life without Him? It is in man's nature to want uninterrupted peace and fulfilment, but it is not part of God's design to let him have it while he lives in sin. Speaking of the troubles of life Elihu says, 'Behold, God works all these things, twice, in fact three times with a man, to bring back his soul from the pit, that he may be enlightened with the light of life' (Job 33v29,30). He does this with Jewish people too — a guilty conscience, doubts and fears about life, dashed hopes, suffering and grief. These are all things that God uses to wake them up to their need to turn back to Him. God speaks to everyone in these ways and they can be a channel for a sensitive and sympathetic presentation of the Gospel.

As a Gentile I have found that when speaking of these things to Jewish people in a day-to-day context the vast majority do not immediately launch into a religious argument which requires a lot of knowledge of Judaism. They tend to assume you do not have such knowledge; rather they will discuss the questions of life using terms with which we are all familiar. Of course, the Jewish details will follow, and the next chapters are to help you with that, but just remember, you already have a lot in common.

3.
From Abraham to the Messiah

It is time to change perspective. We need to look at the things which have moulded the Jewish people and which are distinctive to them. What I have said so far is that though these distinctives are important, they are not more significant than the spiritual and natural things that we all have in common. But remember this, your Jewish friend will not see it that way. Many Jews are so preoccupied with being Jewish that Jewish distinctives are very significant to them. They tend to lose sight of the things we all have in common. Although this is a generalisation, and you will meet Jews who do not fit that description, it remains true for most.

The famous philosopher Hegel once said 'history teaches us that history teaches us nothing.' This is true in the sense that we do not learn from it as we should, but history certainly does teach us. We are all children of our own age, and each age is influenced by those before it. If we study that history, we will understand ourselves better. If we study Jewish history, we will understand the Jews better. Please note the word 'understand'. I am more concerned to give you an understanding that will make you sensitive to your Jewish friend than to equip you with techniques. What follows is vital for gaining that understanding.

Abraham

What is unique about the Jews is that God entered into a covenant relationship with them as a people. It all began with Abram when he lived in Ur around the year 2000 BC, in the region we now call Iraq. His contemporaries were idolaters despite the testimony to the one living God given by men like Shem, the son of Noah, who was still living. God called Abram out of Ur and led him to Canaan to serve Him. He made great promises to him of a land, a multitude of descendants, protection and blessing, and that through him all the earth would be blessed. None of those promises has failed. While making the covenant with Abram, God warned him of difficulties ahead and changed Abram's name to Abraham which means 'father of many nations'. Here are the Jewish roots: a God who works by grace alone and a man who lived by faith alone. Sad to say, like many other peoples today, the Jewish people have forgotten their roots.

Exodus and Settlement

The difficulties of which God warned Abraham occurred in Egypt. When Jacob and his family went there under Joseph's protection it was a deliverance, but later it turned into a captivity through a Pharaoh who saw the Israelites as a threat. Anti-Semitism was born.

We know little of the religious state of the people during their time in Egypt but it probably left a lot to be desired. It is likely that the oppressive measures of Pharaoh were what prevented Israel from settling down in Egypt and becoming 'Egyptians'. In due time it was Moses' task to lead them out to the land where they would be moulded into the people of the LORD, a people of holiness. The memory of that deliverance finds its focus in the Passover night which is observed to this day by multitudes of Jewish people. It has become the main focus of Jewish self-awareness, and its survival is a testimony to the reality of those great events. Israel was free! Free to serve the LORD according to the covenant later made through Moses at Sinai. Sadly, many of them seemed to think they were free to serve themselves, and so God judged that rebellious generation. Only their sons and daughters, together with Caleb and Joshua, settled in the land He had promised.

A Kingdom

After 200 years or so in the land the people wanted a king. Following

Saul's failure, the LORD showed Israel what sort of king pleased Him by anointing David. The reigns of David and Solomon were the high points of Israel's history, during which God gave glimpses of Messiah's as yet future kindom. Anyone who thought that this was the way things were to remain was soon to be disappointed, for the kingdom divided and declined into idolatry in both the north and the south.

The invasions of the Assyrians and the Babylonians led to the people being taken into captivity by 600 BC, and lasting peace and security was never really enjoyed again, despite the return of some after 539 BC. During the remainder of the Biblical period the Jews were always under foreign rule, either by the Persians, the Greeks, the Ptolemies, the Seleucids, or the Romans, except for a period of 100 years under the family of the Maccabees(160-63 BC), who led a revolt against Seleucid rule. This foreign domination was frequently oppressive, with two notable incidents. The attempt of Haman around 470 BC to destroy all the Jews in the Persian empire; and the attempt in 169 BC by the Seleucid ruler Antiochus Epiphanes to root out Biblical religion. Both failed; God had plans for Israel.

The Coming King

The prophets who had warned of the judgements of captivity and foreign domination, and the prophets who actually lived through it, all spoke of better days under the Messiah. We need to remember that such predictions were not as clear to the people of those days as they are to us now, but certain things were unmistakable. God's specially anointed Servant, the King Messiah, would succeed where all others had failed. Under Him all God's people would love righteousness and keep His commandments; their sin would be dealt with, and their enemies vanquished; and the day would come when all the nations would serve the LORD. The Song of Zacharias in Luke's second chapter expresses the ardent longing of an Old Testament believer for all these things. As well as all this the supernatural nature of the Messiah was revealed, and his rejection by many was anticipated. Through prophecies and troubles many in Israel were led to long for the coming Deliverer.

Acceptance and Rejection

The Messianic expectations of men such as Zacharias were not widely held in Jesus' day. For many the hope of independence from Rome was far higher on the agenda than righteousness. Among the religious, the majority were expecting their own righteousness to be confirmed, followed by a reward in Messiah's kingdom. They were not ready for their corruption to be exposed. The powerful were ready to serve Messiah on their own terms, not His. It is not surprising therefore that Jesus met with a mixed reception.

However it is a caricature to see the Jews of that time purely in terms of rejection. If that were true there would be no New Testament Church. We should rejoice that through the preaching of Christ and His Apostles, many in Israel turned from these false hopes and from their sins to faith and righteousness. It was through these Jewish believers that the Gospel was taken to other Jews and also to the Gentiles, so that a new community of faith was formed, one rooted in the history and hopes of Israel; a community which is still growing today.

The rejection of Jesus by the majority of the Jewish leaders was what ensured that the future attitude of the nation to Jesus would continue to be one of rejection. It also ensured that the faithful ones who recognised Jesus as the fulfilment of Israel's hopes would be excluded from national life. Jesus was henceforth to be considered as just another Messianic pretender, and Israel would continue to wait for the promised Messiah. The consequences of this were disastrous. As Christ predicted, foreign armies (the Romans) came and destroyed Jerusalem. Many suffered and many died in those terrible days; and large numbers were led away captive. Nevertheless apostate Israel survived; God had not totally abandoned her.

4.
Exile from Jerusalem

It is very difficult to describe in a few words the subsequent events of Jewish history. What I will try to do is to give a simple summary of the main epochs and events. Although there are many positive aspects to this period, which have had beneficial effects on the Jewish people, it must be remembered that it is a history of exile, with all the deprivation, misery and persecution which that involves.

Moses warned that the land would vomit out those who defiled it, and what greater defilement was possible than the rejection of Him who was full of grace and truth? Hosea 9v12 well expresses the fearfulness of such a judgement, 'woe to them when I depart from them.' This should not be misunderstood to mean that subsequent Jewish suffering has been a judgement on them for the rejection of Jesus by others, those of Jesus' own generation. It has to be seen as a consequence of God's departure from them; a departure which has been neither absolute nor final. Nor should such truth be misused as a justification for anti-Jewishness.

However, although there was much suffering, it should be remembered that it was not woe every minute of the day. There were periods of great cultural achievement and prosperity for the Jews; yet the spectre of suffering and persecution always hovered, and the milestones of Jewish history are frequently ones of persecution.

In the East

Not all Jewish communities outside Israel had their origins in the destruction of Jerusalem in 70 AD. As a result of an earlier exile, and because of trade, Jewish communities have existed in the regions east of Israel since the Babylonian captivity (600 BC) up to the present day, the main centres being in Persia. They were usually free to flourish intellectually and commercially under various rulers, and this situation remained much the same for hundreds of years. Even after 650 AD when the forces of Islam conquered these regions the Jews remained numerous and flourishing, except that they were regarded as second-class citizens and suffered some of the consequences of such a status. In recent times all this has changed dramatically. As Jews from the West began to resettle in Palestine in the 19th century, the Arab and other Islamic nations of the East began to increase the force of the restrictions on their Jewish subjects. As a result a quarter of a million Jews left the eastern communities and settled in Israel between 1948 and 1964. Only a few thousand chose to remain behind.

Under the Roman Empire

The empire of Rome never affected the communities of the East, but by 100 AD her empire had spread all around the Mediterranean and on into Western Europe. Wherever the Romans went they encountered Jewish communities and usually treated them with respect, eventually giving them a privileged status. The destruction of Jerusalem in 70 AD did not really alter this. It was not until the early 4th century, when the Emperor Constantine decided to adopt Christianity rather than persecute it, that things slowly began to change. With the active support of some church leaders, Jewish privileges began to be removed and new restrictions began to be imposed. Fewer choices of occupation were available to Jews, so that they were increasingly limited to the areas of commerce and finance. Conversion to Judaism became illegal. Jews could not have a non-Jewish slave or marry someone who was not Jewish, and new synagogues could not be built. Mob attacks on them became a more frequent phenomenon than in the past.

The account of the spread of Christianity in the Acts of the Apostles makes it plain that opposition from Jewish quarters was a frequent source of tension. What made it particularly difficult for the Church then, and in the 250 years which followed, was that she lacked official status in the eyes of Rome. But the Synagogue was accepted. No doubt this history was a significant factor in the anti-

Jewish developments outlined above, but it does not excuse them. Some of those who suddenly found themselves members of an official faith rather than a persecuted one, took the opportunity to create difficulties for those who had previously caused them considerable distress. Later developments of this anti-Jewishness led to a so-called 'Christian' form of anti-Semitism. This was the deplorable accusation that all Jews were 'Christ-killers', and it was used to justify all kinds of envy, hatred and oppression towards the Jews within the lands of Christendom.

In 400 AD the Roman Empire was divided. One part covered North Africa, Palestine and Syria, and there conditions for the Jewish people remained much the same as they had been, until the Muslim armies invaded most of it at the end of the 7th century. Under Islam the condition of the Jews was marginally improved, so that at times they were free and flourishing but on occasions suffering periods of restriction. This state of affairs continued for many centuries until the resettlement of Palestine began in the 19th century. As already mentioned, the hostile reaction of the Arab and other Islamic nations to this was such that between 1948 and 1964 about 300,000 Jews left this region for Israel.

A significant section of this part of the Roman Empire was not invaded by the Muslim armies until 1453. It became known as the Byzantine Empire, centred on Constantinople, and it continued the oppressive policies against the Jews which had commenced earlier under Rome.

In Europe

In the other part of the Roman Empire, which covered the areas north of the Mediterranean, the authority of Rome disintegrated under the Barbarian invasions of the 5th century. It took until 800 AD before new States emerged, and during this time it seems as if the Jews knew very varied circumstances according to how much local rulers ignored or applied the old restrictions which Rome imposed. One such 'State' was the Holy Roman Empire. In its early days, in the 9th and 10th centuries, the Jews enjoyed new freedoms. This was probably a legacy from the enlightened rule of Charlemagne, whose 8th century reign in central Europe was intelligent and tolerant.

However, this came to an end with the era of the Crusades. These were attempts by 'Christian' noblemen and their subjects, in the 11th and 12th centuries, to win back Palestine from the control of the 'infidel' Muslims. They saw the Muslim presence there as an affront to Christ. But as the Crusader armies headed for Palestine they decided to deal with any 'infidels' they met on the way. This left a trail of Jewish blood as they murdered and pillaged in the Jewish communities which they encountered, often at the incitement of intolerant priests who stirred up 'Christian' anti-Semitism.

Things in Europe were never to be the same after that. The Jews now lived even more separately from their Gentile neighbours, and developed occupations which enabled them to be more mobile in times of emergency. Occupations such as holding public office, farming their own land, and membership of a guild were already forbidden to them, but now there were few rulers who dared have them among their officials. In 1215 the Pope decreed that rulers within Christendom should require their Jews to wear a distinguishing badge. Anti-Jewish events became more common; forced conversions, public disputations, mob attacks, and mass expulsions from one kingdom to another.

The Jews did not experience persecution all the time. Peace and prosperity existed in many places for long periods as wiser rulers saw the value of their Jewish subjects, but the fear of a fresh outbreak was ever present. The most dramatic example of all this was the mixed fortunes of the Jews of Spain. They enjoyed a golden age under Islamic rule from 711 AD until 1146 AD, flourishing in the realms of study, commerce, literature and religion. But the repressions of a subsequent, more fundamentalist Islamic dynasty caused many to flee to the Christian areas in the north of Spain, where they were welcomed. However, when the Christian rulers had succeeded in reconquering the Muslim part of Spain they became less dependant on their numerous and useful Jewish subjects. It was then that the difficulties began. In 1380 the Jews lost many civil liberties, and in 1480 the notorious Inquisition was set up to root out those Jews who had made a superficial profession of Christianity in an attempt to hold on to those liberties. Thousands died in those terrible days, which culminated in 1492 with the expulsion of all Jews from Spain. Portugal followed suit in 1496. A golden era came to an end as 200,000 Jews fled to a variety of destinations such as Holland, Turkey, France, North Africa, and the Americas.

The Jewish experience in Spain was repeated elsewhere in Europe, although not to the same degree. Nowhere else did they flourish so much, nor suffer such a dramatic and wholesale expulsion. It became common in the Middle Ages for rulers to regard the Jews not only as their subjects but also as their property. The more enlightened ones left them alone and generally benefitted from their presence. The greedy looked upon them as a commodity for gain, either by extortion or expulsion.

Italy, the land of the Popes, was the one exception to all this, a surprising fact in that the persecutions usually had a strong religious element. The reason for this was that the Popes did not need the Jews as a source of finance, as merchants, or for literate servants; they had their own Christian ones, and so they left the Jews alone. In England and France periods of prosperity were followed by expulsions in 1290 and 1394 respectively; expulsions which involved the confiscation of most of the Jews' goods. Many of them fled to Germany, which in the Middle Ages was composed of many small states. There they alternately suffered persecution or enjoyed prosperity, but were never expelled en masse.

Poland became a fairly safe haven so that persecuted Jews from all parts of Europe began to settle there. Because of their literacy some Jews joined the middle classes, but many of them simply turned their backs on a world which had rejected them and turned in on themselves. For these people time stood still. They studied the Talmud, the books of Jewish traditional teachings, listened to the Rabbis, and deliberately ignored developments in the wider world. The beneficial effects of the Reformation, and later the Enlightenment, did not spread to those parts of Eastern Europe where most of the world's Jews were living at the beginning of the 16th century. By the late 19th century there were approximately 11 million Jews living in the regions ocupied by the present-day lands of Poland, the Czech Republic and Slovakia, Russia, Hungary, and Romania.

For these Jews conditions gradually got worse. Whenever there was civil unrest the Jews suffered; sometimes as innocent scapegoats, sometimes because of their involvement with the machinery of the government of the day. The Russian Tzars were particularly opposed to them, and confined 5 million Jews to a large area in western Russia between the Black Sea and the Baltic known as the

Pale of Settlement. Compared to rulers elswhere the Tzars sought no gain from the Jews, they simply did not want them, and turned a blind eye to sporadic outbreaks of persecution, much of which was given a 'Christian' justification. After the assassination of Tzar Alexander II in 1881 a series of particularly harsh outbreaks began, later referred to as 'pogroms', which appeared to have had the support of the authorities. This was the straw which broke the camel's back. Three million Jews fled to other parts of the world between the years 1881 to 1914.

Among the many who remained, there was an underlying feeling of hopelessness, which led to a variety of reactions. More began to turn to the mystical Chasidic movement which had emerged in the 18th century as an earlier reaction to oppression; it emphasised joy in God in every area of life, but at the time it was little more than an escape. Today the movement continues among some orthodox Jews, and it has had a noticeable effect on mainstream Judaism. Others raised the banner of a Jewish National Home and became known as Zionists. Still others, like Trotsky, became deeply involved in the revolutionary movements of the day. Despite the apparent hopelessness of the situation many of the devout decided to stay put and wait for the Messiah; He would deliver them.

After the First World War (1918) they had little choice in the matter. The nations began closing their doors to Jewish immigrants; they were trapped. For many of them this meant a terrible fate. When the dust of the Second World War had settled the consequences for the Jews of the Nazi invasion of Eastern Europe were only too clear. Five and a half million of them perished in that terrible butchery. Whether they remained in Eastern Europe because they had chosen to do so, or because they could not gain an entry elsewhere, they were caught in the 20th century's most horrific act of genocide.

Today there are relatively few Jews in Eastern Europe. The largest grouping is made up of the two and a half million who live in the territories which once comprised the USSR. Until recently they were not allowed any form of religious or cultural expression, nor was it easy to emigrate if they wanted to. Now, both are possible.

5.
In the West of Europe

Developments in Western Europe were very different. The twin influences of the Reformation and the Enlightenment gradually produced a different climate of opinion. The Protestant and Puritan principle of freedom of conscience before God meant that Jews who had fled from Spain and Portugal became accepted in Holland as early as 1619, although they initially kept their Judaism a secret. Amsterdam became known as the New Jerusalem as the Jewish community flourished in every area of life, especially in commerce. In 1655 Manasseh ben Israel petitioned Cromwell to readmit the Jews to England, and although Parliament refused, Cromwell's favourable attitude meant that Jews began to come to Britain. By demonstrating that they were valuable members of society, with much to contribute, they increasingly gained acceptance. By 1866 all the civil disabilities of being Jews in a country whose laws assumed a Christian population were removed. In Holland all such disabilities had been removed by 1796.

It was during this period in Holland that the terms *Ashkenazi* and *Sephardi* first began to be used. The earliest Jewish settlers there were from Spain, and they were people of sophistication and education. News of the liberties they were enjoying came to the ears of the oppressed Jews of Poland and Russia, who soon also began to arrive. These Jews had a downtrodden air about them and the Spanish Jews, fearing a loss of privileges, did not make them welcome. They even prohibited intermarriage. Two communities developed, with separate synagogues and social customs, the Spanish one being known as Sephardi and the Eastern European one as

Ashkenazi. The latter soon became the majority and, as it gained influence and respectability, eventually came to stand for the whole community in the eyes of outsiders.

In other parts of Western Europe little change was experienced until after the French Revolution and the conquests of Napoleon. Although the Reformation affected the German Princedoms and the Swiss Cantons, the Puritan principles of freedom did not take root in these countries, and the Jews suffered civil disabilities along with all other minorities. In France, Spain, Austria, Italy, and Belgium the influence of Rome maintained an unchanged 'climate'. The new winds blowing in England and Holland were indeed felt in those countries, but it was not until Napoleon's conquests that circumstances significantly changed. The French Revolution led to the declaration in France, in 1791, of freedom and equality for all, regardless of class, colour or religion. This included the Jews.

The leaders of the Enlightenment thought of freedom for the Jews primarily in humanistic terms, rather than a freedom to practice their own religion; Jewish continuance in Judaism was looked on with disfavour. Freedom was granted nevertheless. Napoleon was looked upon by many as a tyrant, yet as his armies swept through Europe he declared liberty for Jews. His subsequent retreat and defeat caused those liberties to be swiftly withdrawn in most places. However, by 1880, through internal and external pressures, the countries of Western Europe removed all their civil disabilities from the Jews. Only Portugal and Spain delayed until the early years of the twentieth century. The problem was that in many places change occurred superficially, being inspired more by outside pressure than a gradual change of mind. Anti-Semitism was soon to re-emerge in such places, sometimes in frightening proportions.

The Jews were not slow to make good use of these new liberties and, in the 19th century, the Jewish communities of England, Holland, Austria-Hungary and France flourished, and even more so in Germany. For the first time in centuries Jews came to the fore in the arts, politics, business innovation and scientific discovery. Jewish self-help organisations grew rapidly. Reform Judaism, with its sceptical attitude to the Bible and Jewish tradition, emerged at this time in Germany, enabling its followers to assimilate more easily into the surrounding Gentile society. Moses Hess, Theodore

Herzl, and others warned against all this assimilation, urging their people to recognise their nationhood and look for a homeland of their own. They received scant sympathy in the West, because most of the Jews were anxious to be seen as belonging to the nations in which they lived. Any emphasis on Jewish nationhood would only exaggerate their distinctiveness, giving rise to anti-Semitism. The unfolding of events was soon to show how futile such attitudes were.

The nations of western Europe undoubtedly benefitted from the presence of the Jews, and were generally favourable towards them. However, when things went wrong, or threatened to do so, then the Jews became a target of abuse. In the late 19th century public resentment was fuelled when some Jews in Germany and France were involved in financial scandals. Another notorious case was the conviction in France of Captain Dreyfus on a charge of espionage. His subsequent acquittal did nothing to dampen the latent anti-Semitism which the whole affair had brought to the surface. A fear of being flooded with immigrants caused the British Parliament to pass an Aliens Bill in 1905 which resticted the numbers allowed into the country.

These events might have passed unnoticed if it were not for the emergence of a new view of the Jews, coupled with the turn of events in Germany. The new thinking, based on the theory of evolution, insisted that race was a key factor in personal behaviour. In 1873 Wilhelm Marr first put this idea forward in Germany to explain what he believed was an evil trait in Jewish character; a trait which made Jews dangerous to others. Marr coined the term Anti-Semitism to explain and justify dislike for the Jews. This thinking soon caught on, even among the cultured and well educated. The turn of events in Germany was their defeat in the First World War, followed by economic depression. These left a spiritual vacuum which Hitler and the Nazis exploited. Their assertion of the racial superiority of the Germans, as Aryan people, coupled with their promise of a 1,000 year Reich, was received with relief and enthusiasm by many. Their manifesto blamed the Jews for most of the nation's ills, and they asserted that Germany would only be strong again when she broke the influence of the racially inferior Jews. The oppression of the Jews began, and many fled.

The outbreak of the war in 1939 and the subsequent German conquests gave Hitler a free hand to do whatever he wanted with the

Jews in Nazi-occupied Europe. He killed all he wished. The five and a half million who perished in the east of Europe have already been mentioned, a further half a million who had been living in the west also died. A Jewish author termed this appalling destruction 'The Holocaust', a word derived from the Greek for a whole burnt offering. Nowadays it is increasingly referred to as 'The Shoah', a Hebrew word for desolation, destruction, or tempest. Its awesome proportions loom over Jewish history and experience until the present time. The scars it has left in the lives of many are barely healed. It may seem strange to speak of this period as having any beneficial consequences, but the new stimulus it gave to the establishing of a national homeland could be looked at in such a way. The Zionist movement received fresh impetus, and the world-wide sympathy generated by the Holocaust made it difficult to resist the further resettlement of Palestine, although some did try.

Since 1945 Jews have continued to live in western Europe, chiefly in Britain and France, where there are 360,000 and 700,000 Jews respectively. They enjoy full civil liberties and contribute significantly to the social and economic life of the societies of which they are a part. However, Jews set little store by the present peace. They may be content to make use of it, but they know full well that things could change rapidly. The increasing antipathy toward Israel throughout the world is presently creating unease in the Jewish communities of Europe.

6.
Jews in the Americas and elsewhere

Many of the events related above led Jews to settle elsewhere. I have not mentioned this earlier as it deserves its own account. The first Jews to arrive in the Americas came to South America, but not voluntarily. They were banished from Spain and Portugal as a punishment for being Marranos — Jews who had made a profession of Christianity but who secretly practised Judaism. After that Jewish emigration to the Americas was all voluntary: a search for a better life. The earliest of such Jews to arrive were those who sailed with Christopher Columbus in 1492, but along with the rest of the crew, they seem to have been uncertain as to where they were! After that Jewish travellers across the Atlantic made no mistakes of that kind.

In the 17th and 18th centuries there was a steady influx of Jews to the colonies of North and South America. They settled happily in the English and Dutch colonies, but were made to feel unwelcome, and were sometimes persecuted, in the Spanish, Portugese and French dominions. They were mostly traders, especially the Dutch Jews, who played a significant role in the prosperity of the Dutch empire in the 17th century. Their adherence to Judaism was firm, and every community had its synagogue. This was generally respected, and they soon became appreciated members of the newly emerging societies of their adopted colonies.

The reasons why Jews were attracted to such places should be clear when you remember why those settlements first began. The English colonies in particular started off as havens from religious persecution in the mother country. This meant that from the beginning they had laws and charters which allowed civil liberties for all. The Jews were accepted and understood in such places. The puritan principle of liberty of conscience led to Jews being treated as equal citizens for the first time in centuries. The Constitution of the USA, with its many guarantees of freedom, was built upon this principle. All this has led to the USA being a country with few, if any, landmarks of anti-Semitism.

The early days of the 19th century saw Jews in the USA moving westwards with the settlers. They were mostly pedlars and traders, and the stores established by some of them have now become household names, such as Gimbel's and Macy's. In Canada, Jews were active in opening trading posts along the Great Lakes and the St. Lawrence river. All this made the practice of traditional Judaism very difficult, so when some German immigrants arrived with their new and more liberal synagogue tradition it found a ready acceptance. This led to the establishing of the Reform Synagogue movement, and it came to dominate the American Jewish communities by the end of the 19th century.

Another feature of Jewish community life at this time was the emergence of many charitable societies to help the new Jewish immigrants. I mentioned earlier the persecution of the Jews in Russia between 1880 and 1914. Most of the two and a half million who fled went to the USA, (although some went to South America, mostly to Argentina and Brazil.) This enormous influx far outnumbered the Jews already there, but a great work was done by Jewish organisations to help them to establish themselves. To begin with most of them stayed in New York, only later moving on to the other major cities.

The new immigrants were mostly traditional in their Judaism and could not accept the new Reform movement. Conservative Judaism arose out of the desire of many to retain as much tradition as possible, while adapting to their new life. A significant minority retained the old ways of eastern Europe and were known as Orthodox. Further immigrations from Europe took place before and after the Second World War when those fleeing the Nazis, or the memory of them, came to both North and South America.

Throughout the Americas there are well organised Jewish communities, which are fully integrated into the societies they have adopted. Many are prosperous and influential, particularly those in the USA. There is little immigration from one community to another, or back to Europe, or over to Israel, although there is a great deal of communication between them all. What actually binds them together will be discussed in some of the following chapters.

Other Jewish Communities

There are flourishing Jewish communities today in South Africa, Australia and New Zealand, whose growth was mostly due to immigrants arriving from Russia between 1881 and 1914, and from Germany and central Europe between 1933 and 1945. In many respects these communities are very similar to those in western Europe and North America.

Small communities of Jews exist throughout the Asian continent, but the origins of some of them are very difficult to trace. The most numerous are those in the eastern regions of the old Soviet Union. Some of these consist of European Jews who fled east to escape the Nazis, while others, in the regions bordering Afghanistan, have a tradition that they originated from the Assyrian and Babylonian deportations. Many of these are now following in the footsteps of similar communities in Persia, Iraq and Afghanistan, and are emigrating to Israel. Other even smaller communities owe their origins to Jewish traders who settled along the old trade routes from the Mediterranean to the Far East. Some of these communities developed along the sea routes via India, China and the Dutch East Indies; others along the overland route through Central Asia into China. Marco Polo observed many such communities in the 13th century, but now the few remaining ones are tiny and often reduced to poverty. In central Africa the Falasha Jews of Ethiopia, whose origins remain obscure, became well known due to the dramatic airlift of many of them to Israel.

When Moses spoke of Israel being scattered from one end of the Earth to the other (Deuteronomy 28v64) he was obviously not using picture-language. The map on page 38 shows the present population of the Jews in the world according to their countries. But the threat of scattering included the hope of a return.

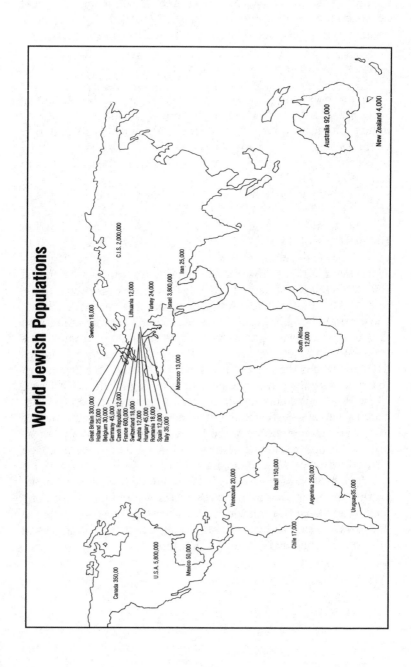

World Jewish Populations

Canada 350,00
U.S.A. 5,800,000
Mexico 50,000
Venezuela 20,000
Chile 17,000
Brazil 150,000
Argentina 250,000
Uruguay 35,000

Sweden 18,000
Great Britain 300,000
Holland 25,000
Belgium 30,000
Germany 45,000
Czech Republic 12,000
France 600,000
Switzerland 18,000
Austria 12,000
Hungary 45,000
Romania 18,000
Spain 12,000
Italy 35,000
Lithuania 12,000
Turkey 24,000
Israel 3,800,000
Morocco 13,000
Iran 25,000
C.I.S. 2,000,000
South Africa 12,000
Australia 92,000
New Zealand 4,000

7.
Return to the land

Any Jewish history book on this subject will quickly remind you
that the Jewish presence in the land of Israel has never ceased. That
is true; so I am going to begin at that point too. In comparison to the
number of Jews in Israel today that presence was a small one, but
they have always been there, and throughout the centuries there
have been those who have returned. 'Next year in Jerusalem!' are
the last words of the Passover, and they express the hope of a
wholesale return to the land, but there have always been some who
went without waiting for that.

After the destruction of Jerusalem by the Roman general Titus in
70 AD, most of the Jews who remained in the land lived in the north,
around Galilee. It was the Emperor Hadrian (about 117AD) who
decided on a policy of rooting-out Judaism. He renamed the land
Palestine and built a Temple to Jupiter in Jerusalem. Jews were
permitted to live anywhere in the land, except Jerusalem, and
Jewish resistance to Rome was ruthlessly suppressed. The Rabbinical Academies were not interfered with by the Romans, and a great
deal of work was done by them in collecting together Jewish
teachings. This collection became known as the Palestinian Talmud.

The invasion of Palestine in 637AD by the armies of Islam made
no great difference to the Jews. They officially became second class
citizens, but in practice their situation depended very much on the
local ruler's attitude. It was during this time that a group of Jewish
scholars completed the insertion of the vowel signs and punctuation
marks in the received Hebrew text, what we call the Old Testament,

which guides our understanding of that text to this day. The conquest of Palestine by the Crusaders from 1099 to 1291 made things very much worse for the Jews. The Crusader aim of bringing the Holy Land under Christian control was achieved by anything but Christian means, and many Jews were massacred as 'Christ-killers'.

Fortunately for the Jews, the Islamic armies, firstly of Saladin and later of the Turks, regained control, and the Jews lived in relative security. From the 13th to the 19th centuries there was a small but steady influx of Jews from Europe, most of whom were escaping persecution. Because some of these were scholars of the mystical understanding of Judaism, a renewed study of Jewish mysticism developed in Palestine, and the town of Safed became a famous centre. The misrule of the Ottoman Turks(1517-1917) left many of the Jews living in the cities of Palestine in poverty and frequently having to rely on outside contributions. If you had visited the land in those days you would have seen a barren, denuded landscape, in which swamps had spread and forests had been destroyed. The cities and villages were largely empty, and brigands roamed; the Palesinian poplation was small. By the end of the 19th century changes had begun which have resulted in the land as we know it today.

Zionism was the name given to the movement which began around the 1860's, with the goal of a Jewish homeland in Palestine. Voices were raised, like those of Theodore Herzl, against the false security of the assimilated Jews in the democracies. In eastern Europe the persecuted Jews knew only too well how insecure they were, and it was from among them that the first settlers began to arrive and purchase land in Palestine in the 1880's. In 1880 there were 24,000 Jews already living in Palestine, but by 1914 the Jewish population had swelled to 90,000. Fifty settlements were established by the new arrivals. However, it was only after 1917, when the British defeated the Turkish forces in Palestine, that the possibility for a homeland under Jewish rule developed. The British had already expressed their sympathy for the idea of the establishment of a Jewish national home in Palestine in the Balfour Declaration of 1917, formulated by the British Prime Minister David Balfour. In the Peace Settlement of 1919 the British were formally apportioned temporary control over Palestine, and the independence which the Jews were then given under British rule led to the rapid creation of a vast array of political, social, agricultural, educational and cultural organisations. The land began to flourish – but so too did the opposition of those inhabitants who felt their concerns were being disregarded.

British sympathy was severly tested as immigration snowballed and the hospility of the Palestinians and the Arab nations began to be felt. Things came to a head in the 1930's and 40's when large numbers arrived from Germany and eastern Europe, so that by 1948 there were 650,000 Jews in the land. Concurrent with all this was the rise of Arab nationalism. Violence was increasigly resorted to and there were rights and wrongs on both sides. In 1948 the British decided to leave. This was not before the United Nations had proposed a partition plan for separate Jewish and Arab states, as a basis for future developments. The Jews accepted it, reluctantly; the Palestinian Arabs did not. This was at a time when there were 980,000 Arabs and 650,000 Jews in Palestine. When the British left in May 1948 the Jews declared the State of Israel, and the Arab nations immediatedly launched a war which aimed to drive them out. They were unsuccesful; and in 1956, 1967, and 1973 Israel suffered further major military hostilities. A measure of peace was achieved in 1978 when Egypt concluded a peace treaty with Israel through the Camp David Accord.

In the early days of the State large numbers of Jews came there from eastern Europe and the Arab lands, swelling the population of Israel to its present figure of 4 million Jews and 3 million Arabs. Throughout her short history she has been subject to numerous terrorist attacks, both at home and against her interests elsewhere in the world. While her sense of insecurity is understandable, and therefore she has needed to retaliate, yet many believe that there have been times when she has gone too far, such as the destructive incursion into Lebanon in 1982, and the lack of sensitivity to the aspirations of Palestinian Arabs which provoked the Intafada.

Today Israel is a thriving nation-state, with the same failures and successes as others. But it is also one full of tensions, and surrounded by enemies. Most of the world's Jews still live elsewhere, and the majority of the Jews who have emigrated there have done so because they were persecuted or had no alternative. It is likely that any large influx in the future will come because of similar regrettable circumstances. The favour with which the world once viewed Israel has seriously diminished, for a variety of reasons, and it has been replaced by indifference or hostility, an example of this being the success of the PLO in 1975 in getting the United Nations to equate Zionism with racism. The increasing influence of Muslim fundamentalism among the Arab nations and especially among Palestinian Arabs, all at the expense of the PLO and more moderate Arab politicians, as well as the influence of the extremists in her own midst, strikes an ominous note for Israel's hopes of peaceful co-existence, despite the Israel-PLO Accord of 1993. Yet however fearful the coming days may appear, we can be sure that all is under the sovereign hand of the God, whose ultimate purpose is to save a people who are loved on account of the patriarchs.

The last five chapters have contained a very brief look at the history of the Jews, which I hope has enabled you to see the wood for the trees. I said at the beginning that you were entering a world which is fascinating and dramatic, although also mundane; containing much suffering, but also great achievements. I hope you have felt something of this, and that you now understand your Jewish friend better. It may be that he has a deep knowledge of it all, or he may have next to none; no matter, he has been moulded by it. History has created in Jewish people certain distinctive characteristics, some of which you may have already observed for yourself.

What are these distinctives? And how do they affect your witness? The next eight short chapters aim to answer those two questions by looking at the effects of all this history on the Jewish people.

8.
The Jews and God

The Jews are unique among the peoples of the world. They alone have been specially formed into a nation by God. That means that when Jews look to their roots they see God. The history books of other nations may be fascinating, and God's providence is there; but the historians are many and the interpretations are varied. Jewish history in the Biblical period is quite different. As we have seen, it began with God, and in it God was always active and revealing what He was doing. It is all written down in the Old Testament Scriptures which are read in the Synagogue to this day.

Because of all this there is no room for doubt, only rebellion. Sadly, the Jews have been as good at that as anyone else. Despite all this history there are Jewish agnostics, Jewish atheists, and no shortage of different Jewish opinions on what God is like, regardless of what the Scriptures might say. Nevertheless it is a fact of Jewish experience that *the idea of God is very difficult to erase from Jewish mentality.* The perennial popularity of books on people's backgrounds and origins, like Alex Hayley's 'Roots', shows how much people want to discover their origins in history; it is an aspect of feeling secure. For Jews those origins are in God; this is not easily ignored, and for some it exerts a powerful influence.

This can be clearly seen in Jewish stories. The first story is one which shows how God's dealings with the Jews has exerted a very strong grip on the thinking of some of them, producing a reverence for God.

'It happened that when a Rabbi Samuel went to Rome, he chanced to find a bracelet belonging to the Queen. A crier went about the kingdom and announced: 'whoever returns the bracelet within thirty days shall receive such and such a reward, but if it is found upon him after thirty days his head will be cut off.' But the Rabbi waited until after the thirty days, and then he returned it. The Queen asked 'Did you not hear the proclamation?' He answered, 'Yes.' So she said 'Then why did you not return it within thirty days?' 'In order,' he answered, 'that you should not say that I feared you, for I returned it only because I feared God.'

That one was serious, but this second one is typically humorous. 'Mr. Abrahams, driven to desperation by the endless delayings of his tailor who was making him a pair of trousers, finally cried, "Tailor, in the name of heaven it has already taken you six weeks!" "So?" "So, you ask? Six weeks for a pair of trousers? It took God only six days to create the whole universe!" "Huh" shrugged the tailor, "look at it…"'

I do not know about you, but I cannot help laughing at that. Yet the words of the tailor reflect some very wrong attitudes. God's existence is certainly taken for granted; He cannot be ignored; but there is a lack of confidence in what He does. There is even a tendency to blame God for evil. It is almost as if the storyteller feels trapped; wanting to escape from God, but finding himself unable to do so. Many Jews feel like that, and it is because they are puzzled by their fate in history. God cannot be excluded from their thinking, even in times of hardship, but it is often easier to joke about things rather than face up to what God actually says about them in the Bible. The idea of God is very difficult to erase from the thinking of Jewish people.

I remember talking with a Jewish atheist and, at one point in the discussion, asking him, 'What do you as an atheist make of being Jewish?' I was trying to get him to face the reality of God in his history. He knew what I was getting at and replied 'Oh yes, I've come to terms with that now; I've sorted that out.' English or Chinese atheists do not find that their nationality confronts their atheism, but Jewish atheists do, it is something that has to be 'sorted out'. Most Jews are not atheists, and it is their history which keeps them from such rank unbelief. It is important to bear this in mind when witnessing to a Jewish friend.

This relationship of God to the Jews was first expressed by Him in terms of a covenant, 'I will be your God, and you will be my people.' It is a special committed relationship. All the Biblical history at the beginning of the previous chapter is based on that. God has created them, and God has kept them. It has produced in Jewish people *a strong sense of togetherness and a sense of destiny*. Whether Jews believe in God or not they feel this bond. In fact I have had serious discussions on Messianic prophecy with quite godless Jewish people in which they have defended the Jewish view as if they believed it! With a Rabbi they would express their unbelief; with me they stand alongside their people. It is a strong sense of solidarity. You can therefore expect that your first attempts to witness will be seen as a threat to this togetherness. Just be patient.

It is important to ask at this point in what sense God is still the God of Israel, because it will affect your approach to witness. In Paul's day two great changes came about that caused him to pose the question, 'Has God cast away His people?'(Romans 11v1) One change was that, compared to the days immediately after Pentecost, only a few Jews were believing in Jesus. Another was that a new body of faith had emerged, made up of Jews and Gentiles. As a nation central to God's purposes the Jews appeared to be fading out of the picture. In fact Jesus had made it plain that this would happen when He said to the Jewish leadership, 'The kingdom of God shall be taken from you, and given to a nation bringing forth the fruits of it.'(Matthew 21v43) The great change was that the kingdom of God in the world was no longer confined to a nation, the Jews. Its new form was that of a community of faith, a spiritual nation, composed of Jews and Gentiles who trust Jesus, called in the New Testament, the Church.

But this does not mean that the promises which God made to the nation of Israel are of no relevance today. Paul still refers to Israel as 'his(God's) people', and this is because of the covenant with Abraham, as he wrote in Romans 11v28 'as far as the election is concerned they (the Jews) are loved on account of the patriarchs, for God's gift and his call are irrevocable.' This means that God will keep them as a people, and yet use them in His purposes. As far as our evangelism is concerned it means that they are to be called to faith through the Messianic promises God gave to them. Their unbelief does not mean that they are an ethnic group like any other, to be evangelised like ignorant pagans. A comparison of Paul's approach to the Jews in Antioch (Acts 13:13-41) with his approach to the pagans of Athens (Acts 17:22-34) illustrates this point. It is the same Gospel, but presented differently to those who had the promises and those who did not. Those promises are still held out to the Jews today, and that affects the way we present the Gospel to them. Religious Jews in particular identify with God's promises to them through Abraham, Moses, and the Prophets, and even the less religious Jews feel it is all their history. It is quite right for them to do this, even though they are ignoring the fact that God has withdrawn His kingdom from them.

This awareness of being God's people has meant that *Jews assume a favourable standing with God.* They do not think of being 'saved' as Christians do. They are already OK. After all, they reason, why did God make them His people if He was not generally pleased with them? This false confidence has to be undermined by using the law of God to show them their sin and guilt, and by showing them that their promised Messiah was sent to save them from their sins.

Another consequence of their being God's people is that in our witness we must learn to *provoke Jews to jealousy.* Paul wrote that salvation has come to the Gentiles so as to provoke the Jews to jealousy(Rom 11v11). Just what does he mean? Perhaps it will become clear if we remember that envy and jealousy are not the same. Your friend takes out an attractive girl whom you like; you may be envious but you cannot be jealous, unless she is first 'your' girlfriend. Jews should not only envy Gentile Christians because of the blessings of God which they are enjoying, but they should also be jealous of them, because what Christians are enjoying was promised to the Jews in the first place! We are enjoying what is theirs.

Paul put it like this, 'Jesus Christ has become a servant to the circumcision (the Jews) for the truth of God, to confirm the promises made to the fathers.'(Romans 15v8) God made definite promises to them: of a personal relationship with Himself, forgiveness of sins, spiritual life, and the assurance of life after death. Religious Jews hope for such things, but do not experience them, and most Jews are impressed by them even if they make little or no effort to obtain them. But for you they are a present reality with the full revelation of God through His Son, Messiah Jesus. What could be more glorious!

But most Jews think of Christianity as an offshoot of Judaism which went wrong by coming under Gentile pagan influence. So, it is vital that as you witness to all this blessing from God you make

it plain that *what you believe is rooted in God's dealings with Israel.*
God revealed His righteous character at Sinai and in judgements like
the Babylonian captivity. Is He not the same today? Calvary
certainly demonstrates His determination to judge sin. The Passover
and the Temple sacrifices exhibited His mercy for His people
through the death of a substitute; did not Calvary do the same as the
fulfilment of those things? . They will only be provoked to jealousy
if we make it plain that what we believe is very Jewish. You should
make it plain that *your God is the God of Israel,* and that you are
enjoying all the things that God promised to Israel — things which
He predicted would be shared with the Gentiles. This means you
should *use the Old Testament as much as possible* to demonstrate
what you believe (Jews call it the Tanakh). And when you use the
New Testament make sure that your friend realises that *the New
Testament is a very Jewish book,* a book written by Jews about Jesus
the Jew, whose first followers were all Jews. Edith Schaeffer aptly
draws attention to all this in the title of her book, 'Christianity is
Jewish'. We want Jewish people to realise that we are calling them
back to the God of Israel, who made covenants and promises with
their forefathers; the One who has richly blessed us in Jesus the
Messiah.

9.
The Jews and Jesus

If there is one expression I have heard time and time again when witnessing to Jewish people it is this one, 'But you can't be Jewish and believe in Jesus.' It has become so ingrained in Jewish mentality that Jesus is not the Messiah, that rejection of Jesus is considered an essential part of Jewishness. It is a Jewish distinctive; an effect of Jewish history upon the Jews. If a Gentile wants to convert to Orthodox Judaism in Britain there is a preliminary interview with a board of Rabbis to discover if it is worth entering upon the long procedure that is necessary. In that preliminary interview one of the first questions is 'Do you believe Jesus is the Son of God?' If the candidate has any hesitation in denying this then he is automatically ruled out. You cannot be a Jew and believe in Jesus.

In an American book 'The Jewish Almanac' there is a chapter on false Messiahs, but remarkably Jesus is not even mentioned. Did the authors make a mistake? Hardly! Their readers may have been ignorant of the nine names mentioned in the Almanac, but they would not have been ignorant of Jesus. So there was no need to even mention Him! This deep-rooted rejection of Jesus is immensely sad for the Christian to observe in Jesus' own people; a sadness which is deepened by recalling that here is a people rejecting or almost totally ignoring its most famous son, while many in the rest of the world admire Him. The fact that it will be to their own eternal loss makes everything far worse.

Of course there are variations on the way this rejection is expressed. Among the Reform and Liberal Jews there is a tendency to admire Jesus. Summarising their views Shalom Ben-Chorin wrote, 'The modern Jewish image of Jesus is far more positive than the medieval one. Not only is the historicity of Jesus rarely denied, but much of the gospel material is readily accepted. More problematic for Jews are the gospel accounts of Jesus' death and resurrection as well as the special consciousness and power attributed to him.' Among such Jews we can see that a new respect has emerged, but the old rejection of His claims is still plain. This respect is shared by the irreligious, such as Albert Einstein, who said 'I am a Jew, but I am enthralled by the luminous figure of the Nazarene.....No one can read the gospels without feeling the actual presence of Jesus. His personality pulsates in every word. No myth is filled with such life.' Among the Orthodox the attitude is more ostrich-like, and is expressed by Michael Asheri in his book 'Living Jewish'. 'We know he(Jesus) lived and have a vague idea of what he preached but there it ends. The widespread idea that the Jews, while rejecting Jesus' claims to divinity, consider him a great teacher and moral figure is completely false. We do not accept his claims and are oblivious to his teachings; we are simply not interested in him or in what he had to say, any more than Christians are interested in Mohammed.'

Since the beginning of this century there has been a more sophisticated expression of this rejection which attempts to avoid the tensions over Jesus. It is especially popular today. Rather than ignoring Jesus or dismissing Him with faint praise, there are those Jews who try to come to terms with the fact that Jesus' teaching has done a lot of good. Jesus has been good for the Gentiles; in fact, they would say, He is their way back to God. But not so for the Jews; they are already with God through the covenant made with Abraham. They do not need Jesus. This sometimes goes by the name of 'Two Covenant Theology'. This idea is clearly denied by many New Testament statements that Jesus is the only way to the Father, but if your Jewish friend brings it up it may be better to argue from the Old Testament first of all. The words 'Not Yet' hang over the whole Old Testament. From Abraham onwards there is a looking forward to God's promised salvation; it had not yet arrived. The sacrifices, which were essential for approaching the LORD, illustrated this most poignantly. Their very repetition showed that they were not actually propitiating God's wrath against sin (see Heb.9v25-10v4). Jeremiah made it plain that that would only be achieved under a new covenant (Jer. 31v31-34). How then could any earlier covenants save?

For Israelis who feel this need to come to terms with Jesus there is an extra factor to take into account. Jesus is not an 'alien'; He was born and brought up there too. Ferdinand Zweig put it like this, 'Being confronted with Jesus in this way (in Israel) is a new experience to the Jew. In the Diaspora Jesus looked alien to the Jew. But in Israel he is seen as the Jew from Nazareth, a native of this country, a Sabra, with claims to the land as strong as any. He cannot be brushed aside as a foreign influence.' Now please do not run away with the idea that all Israelis are falling over themselves to become believers, but it is a significant point of difference which can be used when witnessing to Israelis, of whom there are many outside of Israel.

As I have indicated, all this rejection is very much an inherited position; it is an effect of Jewish history. It stems from the initial rejection of Jesus by the Jewish leadership, and this needs to be clearly understood. Other factors have certainly come in and have increased the tension, but this is where it all began. Because of this the principal reasons for rejecting Jesus as Messiah remain the same today as they were then. Jesus claimed equality with God in saying that He was the Son of God. He was condemned for this on the grounds that it was blasphemy, and His subsequent crucifixion appeared to confirm this verdict. But then He rose from the dead. The Apostles proceeded to explain how His death was a sacrifice for sin and God's only way of forgiveness. Nevertheless, this was firmly rejected by the Jewish leadership. Man's need of spiritual rebirth from above was also unacceptable, along with God's grace as the foundation of all our hopes of salvation.

It does not take much spiritual perception to see man's pride and unbelief as the underlying factor in all this rejection. The same pride and unbelief which caused Israel to turn away from God time after time in the Old Testament period, led to His rejection when He was among them in the flesh. It is the same for all men, for you and for me. The Jewish expression of this rejection is especially strong because they of all people were so directly confronted with the truths of God incarnate and a suffering Saviour. As Jewish identity can only be fulfilled in the belief of these things, so it is inevitable that the rejection of them will lead to that rejection becoming basic to the identity of Jews who do not believe. This is what accounts for the strange fact that there is really only one thing which unites all Jews. It is not Judaism; neither is it Zionism; it is that Jews do not believe in Jesus. Those who do are no longer considered Jews.

There are a few practical conclusions we can draw from all this. You should *expect an initial rejection of your testimony* about Jesus, and that it may be forcibly expressed. However you should recognise that this is unlikely to be a thought-out response to a serious examination of the facts. It is the expression of an inherited position, by which your friend shows his solidarity with his people. Be prayerful and patient! Begin to show from the Old Testament that these truths are taught there; it is not some new set of dogma invented by Gentiles. One young lady I knew came to faith after observing the family Passover. She realised that what her Christian friends had been saying to her was not an alien thing, but was right in line with the Biblical elements of the Passover story.

Furthermore you should recognise that *a true conviction of sin is your friend's primary need.* When he has experienced this he will not be so quick to assert that he has no need of a new birth, or a sacrifice for his sin, or a Divine Messiah to make that sacrifice for him. He will be glad of it! It is no good arguing someone into the ground about these truths, especially Messianic prophecy, if they do not see and feel why they are so important - that is, because of our hopelessness in sin. Keep that firmly in mind, and pray that the Lord will open their eyes to it. Pray too that He will help you to speak boldly. It is not easy to speak one to one with a friend about his sins, but it has to be done. Then you can go on to speak of Jesus, the Saviour.

10.
The Jews and Judaism

The title of Lionel Blue's recent book is about the best twelve word summary of Judaism you will find: 'To Heaven With The Scribes And Pharisees. The Jewish Path To God'. Jesus got it wrong; the Scribes and Pharisees were right. Judaism today is the child of the Scribes and Pharisees, and because of this you do not have to read specialist books on it to gain an understanding of its spirit; it is all before you in the pages of the Gospels. However it is useful to know more than just the spirit of things, and that is what I want to look at with you now.

Our Lord's parable of the Pharisee and the Tax Collector shows us that, in essence, the Pharisees were self-righteous. Much of their doctrine was orthodox, but their practice was one of a works-righteousness before God. From earliest times Moses had to warn against this tendency, 'the LORD your God is not giving you this land to possess because of your righteousness, for you are a stiff-necked people'(Deut. 9v6). Judging by the words of a modern orthodox author, Rabbi Arye Forta, the lesson has still not been learnt, 'The key to a meaningful relationship with God is righteousness, and the capacity for righteousness is within each individual human being'(Jewish Chronicle, 30th October 1987). This misunderstanding is not unique to the Jews, it is a consequence of sinful human pride.

The preaching of Christ and the Apostles offered Israel a righteousness with God through faith in Jesus, but many of the Pharisees rejected this. They preferred their own way, *a religion of righteousness by works*. Today's Judaism is the heir of this rejection; it is a further effect of Jewish history upon the Jews. Spiritually it has been a devastating one.

How was it that the thinking of the Pharisees came to dominate the Jewish scene? They were certainly not the only religious grouping in Israel in the first century AD. What was it that enabled them to come to prominence? The main reason was that after the destruction of the Temple in 70 A.D. the synagogues became the focus for Jewish community life, and it was there that the Pharisees were already taking the lead. Their antagonism to the believers in Jesus was such that, despite the large numbers of those believers, they eventually succeeded in excluding them from the synagogues. They did this around the end of the first century AD by inserting a 'blessing' in the liturgy which required the worshipper to curse heretics, and there appears to have been a specific reference to Jewish Christians in this.

The result of all this was that the Pharisees defined Jewishness and the Jewish religion in the post-Temple era; and that included the rejection of Jesus as Messiah. I believe the day will come when this will change. Paul wrote 'all Israel will be saved'(Romans 11v26), and our Lord said to the Jewish leadership 'you will see me no more until you say 'Blessed is he who comes in the name of the LORD!'' (Matthew 23v38,39). I believe this means that the day will come when great numbers in Israel, including the leaders, will believe in Jesus. Then there will be so many Jews believing in Jesus that that belief will be seen as a chief characteristic of Jewishness! The Jewish world will be turned upside down. In the meantime we face a different situation, one in which the Rabbis equate Jewishness with Judaism.

One of the great sources of conflict between our Lord and the Scribes and Pharisees was the matter of their traditions. These were binding observances which they had added to the laws of Moses, and which were meant to encourage the keeping of those laws by preventing people from infringing the actual Mosaic commands. In time, the weight of these traditions became a great burden and frequently opposed the spirit of the law. An example can be found in Mark 7v9-13 where the Scribes' and Pharisees' tradition on vows actually involved breaking the fifth commandment.

In Jesus' day the traditions were transmitted orally, but it eventually became necessary to write them down. Subsequent to this many Rabbis made comments on what was written, and finally it was all gathered together around 500 AD and became known as the *Talmud*. It is about the same size as the Encyclopedia Britannica, and pious Jews devote more time to studying this than the *Tanakh* (the Jewish term for the Old Testament Scriptures.)

Today the Talmud is the main authority for Jewish practice and belief, and it is the Rabbis' task to teach it. I deliberately mention practice before belief because that is what predominates in Judaism. *As the heir of the Scribes and Pharisees, Judaism is a religion of tradition.* If you have not already heard the song 'Tradition' in the musical 'Fiddler on the Roof' you should do so, it is as good an illustration of this fact as you will get. There have been revolts against this burden of tradition, such as the Karaites who only acknowledge the Tanakh, and the modern movements for reform which pick and choose which traditions to observe, but none of these has succeeded in removing the Talmud from centre stage. In fact such movements are of the same spirit as the Talmud since they still foster a self-righteous attitude. The next few paragraphs tell you something of the four main groupings within Judaism today.

Orthodox

Orthodox belief holds the Scriptures to be the infallible Word of God, and orthodox practice is based on the Talmud. The role of the Rabbi is to interpret the Talmud for modern life, but not to depart from it. The main services for worship take place in the Synagogue on the Sabbath (Saturday), although there are also daily services and special ones on holy days. The services are in Hebrew, and are mainly made up of prayers, praises and Scripture readings, according to a set pattern. In the Synagogue the men and women sit separately. If you wish to visit a Synagogue you are free to do so, but you would be wise to let the Rabbi know you are coming, and to ask him if someone could sit with you to guide you through the service. The synagogue is also a centre for study. Within orthodoxy great stress is laid on family life, and the Sabbath meal (Friday night) is the highlight of the week. The Sabbath begins on Friday evening, at sunset, and ends on Saturday evening.

Most Jews in Britain today would call themselves orthodox because they are members of an orthodox Synagogue, but this does not mean that they conform to all I have written above; far from it.

Only about 2% regularly attend a Synagogue. Few believe the Scriptures are God's Word or trouble to keep very many of the traditions in their daily life. However, most would keep some of the traditions. For this reason many use the word 'traditional' to describe such Jews, who call themselves orthodox but are not practising. You may wonder why they bother to belong to a Synagogue at all. What I have written earlier should answer that for you; it is the need and desire to stick together. But it also a very practical matter; synagogue membership is necessary if a Jewish person is to be buried in a Jewish cemetery, and that is very important for virtually all Jews.

Chasidic

This is a tiny grouping, yet its adherents are the ones who are often seen in photographs which portray religious Jews. The origins of this movement are in the 18th century, and it has since divided into a number of sects which appear similar to the outsider. Chasidic Jews are orthodox in their beliefs, but due to the circumstances of hardship in which the movement began they have some distinctive emphases. These include devotion in prayer, song and dance as a means of expressing joy and arriving at ecstasy, and faith in their leader, the Tzaddik or Rebbe. It is a movement which stresses the significance of every member, and this explains something of its popularity. It can be summed up as a movement which sought to put soul into the practise of Judaism. Scholarship was not enough, mystical fervour and burning enthusiam were to be aimed at. Needless to say, its adherents are marked by great zeal. Their strong streak of mysticism, which sometimes borders on the occult, always makes them difficult to reason with.

It is worth noting that although they were originally branded as heretical, they are now viewed with growing acceptance by the Jewish establishment. This is especially so of the Lubavitch group, who are very influential in promoting a zeal for Judaism within the Jewish community. This meets with mixed reactions; some hold them in awe, while others dislike them intensely. Many Jews like someone to be devout, but not if the devout try to make them devout too! As you can imagine, the Lubavitch group are particularly opposed to any efforts at evangelising Jews.

Reform

This movement began in Europe in the 19th century, and was inspired by the desire to accomodate Judaism to modern life. The Jews were then becoming freer to take part in the life of society at all levels, but many believed that they could not do so if they remained in orthodoxy. Therefore they rejected the Talmud as binding, and only practiced what they felt was relevant to a modern society. For example, two obvious differences to someone visiting their synagogues would be the men and women sitting together, and the use of the national language as well as Hebrew. They also accepted liberal thinking on the Bible, and so rejected the Tanakh as the Word of God. They have retained the same stress on synagogue worship and family life.

Although they account for only 10% of the Jewish community in the UK, their synagogue members are usually more committed than 'traditional' Jews because they have taken a conscious step away from orthodoxy. They are usually more friendly towards Christians, though not necessarily more open to the Gospel.

Liberal and Progressive

This is another small grouping which can be described as similar to Reform, but having an even more liberal approach. They are part of the same movement, but they have taken things further, and therefore reject more of the traditions. For example, larger parts of their services are conducted in English.

A move to the right characterises many areas of life today, and Judaism is also experiencing this. Because of this the Reform and the Liberal and Progressive movements are often indistinguishable as they both return to more traditional ways. An increasing number of young Jews, disillusioned with materialism, are turning to orthodox Judaism to give them a purpose in life. These are sometimes referred to as 'born-again Jews'.

In other parts of the world different names may be used for these groupings within Judaism but you will find the same basic types. There will always be the orthodox who stick to traditonal ways and beliefs, although there will be many differences in practice, from the devout to the 'traditional'. Chasidic Jews can be met with in most countries where there is a Jewish community. Jews who are convinced that the traditions and the Scriptures are not of divine origin, and therefore not binding in every detail, are found everywhere. But there will be differences of proportion. For instance, in the USA the numerically dominant group is called 'Conservative', which in practice is similar to the 'Orthodox' in Britain, but they do not accept the final authority of either the Scriptures or the Talmud. The 'Orthodox' group in the USA is relatively small and characterised by a greater devotion than its British namesake. The one term 'Reform' covers the 'Reform' and the 'Liberal and Progressive' in Britain.

An overview

If we take an overview of all this, we can say that *when it comes to religion, Jews fall into the categories of careless, social, and devout.* The majority are careless; they like to think Judaism is around but they do not practise it, they are either indifferent or simply too busy. A large number are involved in Judaism for its social value; the synagogue and its many social functions is a way of life for them. A minority actually relate it all to God in their thinking, and as they follow the practices of Judaism they are sincerely seeking to do God's will.

The important practices of Judaism

It is not necessary for you to know about too many holy days, ceremonies and traditions, but I will mention those with which all Jews are familiar. This will not only give you an understanding of your friend's religious background, but will also provide you with one means of presenting the Gospel.

Circumcision at eight days for the Jewish boy is a universally practised ceremony. At the age of thirteen Jewish boys take part in a *Bar Mitzvah* (son of the commandment) ceremony, in which they read a portion of the law of Moses, usually in the Synagogue service on the Sabbath. They are then considered to be spiritually adult and responsible to keep God's law. The ceremony is often followed by a big social celebration. Some synagogues hold a similar ceremony for girls, called a *Bat Mitzvah,* held at the age of twelve.

The *Sabbath meal* on Friday evening is an important family occasion for the many Jews, and the *Sabbath* which follows is taken seriously by the more devout as a day for rest and Synagogue attendance. Nowadays only a few keep the *kosher food laws.* These laws are related to the Mosaic regulations on clean and unclean foods, and they stipulate special methods of slaughter, and what may and may not be eaten. However most Jews do know about them, and will probably feel that they ought at least to avoid pork. The *Passover meal, or Seder,* is a great family occasion when many relatives will be invited. It is a bit like Christmas lunch in so far as it is the main festive occasion and family get together of the year. But it contains much religious ceremony which is prescribed in a set book called a *Haggadah.*

The main Synagogue occasion of the year is the *New Year and the Day of Atonement (Rosh Hashanah and Yom Kippur).* This is in September/October and marks the moment when Jews believe that their actions of the past year are judged, their sins forgiven, and their life for the next twelve months is fixed. By engaging in repentance in the ten days between the New Year and the Day of Atonement they hope to secure forgiveness for the past year and blessings for the next. Yom Kippur involves a day of fasting and Synagogue attendance. This draws far larger Synagogue attendances than usual, up to 30% of the community will be there. It is worth pondering why this should be so. Two festivals which are particularly popular are *Purim,* which celebrates the deliverance of the Jews recorded in the book of Esther, and *Chanukkah,* which celebrates their deliverance from fierce persecution in 165BC. The children are especially involved in these two festivals.

There is an observation on all this which I must underline to you if you have not already made it. Jewish people think of their religion very much in terms of practice, and by contrast, they view Christianity as a religion which is more concerned with belief. Most Jews will see the differences between the various synagogue types in terms of their practice, not their doctrines. Because of this they do not think that God is so worried about all the differences of belief in the world, as long as we live good lives. I remember talking with a family on their doorstep, and when I mentioned that God was a person whom we could know they expressed surprise. Although they were regular attenders at an Orthodox synagogue this was not what they believed about God; however they were accepted because they practised all the right things. This sort of thing could never be acceptable in a true Christian church and it illustrates the difference. A church expects right belief and right practice. From this you can see that from a Jewish perspective there is simply *no need to become a Christian, you just live a good life, and that is all God wants.* This inevitably encourages a self-righteousness, and the Rabbis bear a heavy responsibility for promoting this. It is our task to undermine it from the Scriptures.

There is, however, a beneficial side to this emphasis on good living which we should not fail to notice. The Jewish community is one with a strong emphasis on moral standards and good social behaviour. Those standards are rooted in Biblical teaching and have been encouraged by the Rabbis. Because of this Christians frequently find themselves in sympathy with Jewish norms of behaviour; the Judeo-Christian Tradition is the term often used to describe this common ground. For Jews this means *they are marked by an awareness of moral right and wrong, with a concern to see such standards upheld.* They are also very conscious of the social needs of others, and are frequently active to relieve them as best they can. This is something to be admired in the Jewish community, and Christians should beware of belittling it in their concern to point out the need for God's gift of righteousness in Jesus the Messiah.

11.
The Jews and the Messiah

David Abrahams really wanted a new bike, but his dad could not afford it. However that did not stop him asking from time to time! The reply was predictable though, 'When the Messiah comes, David, when the Messiah comes.' In other words, this year, next year, sometime, never. For many Jews their hopes about the coming of the Messiah are so faint, and so far removed from reality, that his coming is merely a figure of speech for something which is very unlikely to take place at all! That is not so for all Jews. At the other end of the spectrum there are the Chasidic Jews who have car stickers proclaiming, 'We want Moshiach now!' (Moshiach being their pronunciation of the Hebrew for Messiah). They are avidly looking forward to his coming. In the middle are those Jews who have the belief that he is coming, but it does not affect them much because they have not been taught to expect much. So what does Jewish tradition teach Jews to believe about the Messiah?

The important thing to realise in considering this matter is that present Jewish teaching on the Messiah did not emerge from a religious vacuum. It arose from the controversy with Jesus, and subsequently the Jewish believers, in the first century AD. In that century Jewish teaching on the Messiah underwent radical changes by way of reaction to the arguments of Jewish Christians. This reaction has continued down the ages in the confrontation of belief between Christians and unbelieving Jews. It is an effect of Jewish history. Of course, we should not expect that prior to Messiah's coming everything in the Old Testament would be clear to the Jews of those days, although it is remarkable how much was understood. But once He had come, and He and His followers had explained these matters, then to hold to an alternative view became a clear rejection.

First of all it is maintained today that *Messiah is not the Son of God,* at least not in the sense that Christians understand it. He is merely a special human figure, divinely inspired, and with unusual effectiveness for God. His main purpose is to teach Israel and the whole world to obey God, to deliver Israel from their enemies, and to rule over all nations from Jerusalem. He will be of the line of David, a man of vision and with regal authority. Under his rule there will be worldwide peace. The Jews expect the Temple to be rebuilt in his days. The *idea of Messiah as a sacrifice for sin is totally rejected,* although the awareness of him as a sufferer is not ignored. Such a view of the Messiah is confined to what men can understand.

Among the Reform, and also among the Liberal and Progressive Jews, there is a preference for the idea of a Messianic age of peace and justice, brought about by men's efforts, rather than the coming of a special individual.

When speaking to your Jewish friend about the Messiah it is wise to check whether or not he believes in the idea at all. If he says he does not then you can challenge him along various lines, such as those Scriptures which point to a personal Messiah, or that Judaism has always held to such a belief, or by pointing out to him that we obviously need someone special to deal with our problems. If he does believe, then it is good to ask him what he thinks Messiah will be like. Express your agreement where you can, and then go on to ask him what he thinks of various Scriptures of which he has not taken notice. You must make sure it is clear to him why we need a Divine and a suffering Messiah. It is easy to get bogged down in sterile debate and lose a sense of direction in your discussion. I have listed the main prophecies of the Messiah at the end of chapter 16, and some detailed suggestions for dealing with Jewish questions on the Messiah in Appendix 3.

What stands out about Judaism's attitude to the Messiah is the lack of any sense of real hopelessness without him. Some definitely look forward to his coming, but they do not depend on him for salvation. One rabbinical tradition is that he will come when all Jews keep the law for one moment of time. Such an idea obviously did not spring out of a belief in man's hopelessness. It is this self-confidence and self-righteousness which enables Judaism to have such a low view of the Messiah. It comes from the sinful nature which we all have in common.

12.
The Jews and persecution

It is lovely to watch children playing together, they are usually so carefree, imaginative and exciting. But not always. It is disturbing to see the way they can gang up on one another, picking on distinctive features and turning them into a reason for abuse. These things leave their mark, but it is difficult to predict just what that mark will be. For some it strengthens, for some it crushes, while others appear to take little notice, but just keep their distance from those who taunt them. Likewise, persecution has left its mark on the Jews. I have already mentioned the sense of solidarity created because God chose them; *persecution has strengthened this sense of solidarity.* Jewish history has not been one of unrelieved suffering, but the periods marked by suffering are the ones remembered most clearly. This is very understandable, and it has created the belief that they are unwanted by the peoples among whom they live. They may be tolerated, but they are still outsiders.

There is little doubt that without this persecution many more Jews would have assimilated into their surrounding cultures, and the various Jewish communities would be much smaller than they are now. The awareness of this danger of disintegration has produced *an obligation to stick together.* Jewish consciousness that others have persecuted them, and that they are in danger of fading away as a people, results in a strong pressure to stay within the community.

The most significant focus for this is over who to marry. There is great pressure not to 'marry-out' to a Gentile, and the very orthodox will cut-off a son or daughter who does this. With the majority things are not taken so seriously, but life is not therefore without its problems. My daughter asked a schoolfriend of hers to come to a Rainbow Club meeting at our church, but it caused more problems than we anticipated. We then learnt that the father was Jewish and the mother Gentile, and although neither of them was at all religious, nevertheless a lot of tension arose due to pressure from the Jewish relatives not to allow it. They could see another youngster being lost to the community and they mustered as much opposition as they could. This fear of assimilation leads Jewish communities to spend a lot of money and energy on youth clubs. The activities are little different from those at any other club, but it keeps them together and will hopefully lead to them marrying a Jewish partner. In point of fact, most Jewish youngsters want to marry someone Jewish, but the adults prefer to err on the side of caution!

If you have suffered from being laughed at because of having big ears or flat feet then you will no doubt become sensitive if the conversation turns to such things! Jewish people feel like that when 'Jews' start to be discussed. However favourable the discussion may appear to be, they are always ready for the 'but'. *Jews have an understandable sensitivity to criticism.* They are so familiar with being the scapegoat for the failures of others, that they find it difficult to accept any comment as well meaning, especially if it is expressed publicly. It may surprise you to know that some are even cautious about having their good points mentioned too much. When Harold Macmillan made the comment that, whereas once there were a lot of Old Etonians in the British Cabinet, now there were a lot of old Estonians (Jews), he could have been interpreted as speaking favourably of Jewish achievements. Few Jews would receive it that way. References to their strength are often understood as a warning against their influence; after all, that was why Pharaoh persecuted them at the very beginning.

This means that when you speak to someone Jewish about his people you should not use expressions like "you Jews". Or if you speak to him about his sins never refer to them as in some way a Jewish sin. He may be personally greedy, but to then say "of course the Jews have all the money don't they", is not only untrue, but also hardly calculated to win him. It will only provoke anger because it is the language used by the enemies of the Jews when lumping them all together, and then treating them as undesirable. Christians should never use such language because it is the language of stereotype, and we should always treat people as individuals. However you should not hesitate to speak to a Jewish friend of his own sin; Jewish people do not have to be treated like the best bone china, and they will usually respect you for being honest.

A further warning is needed here. You may be tempted to tell Jewish jokes to someone Jewish to create a friendly atmosphere. It will not work! Jews, like all people, tell jokes about themselves as a way of laughing at themselves, but their sensitivity to criticism means that if you do it you will be suspected of having some deep-seated feelings of anti-Semitism.

While we are on the subject of Jewish humour it is worth noting one major aspect of that humour which is due to all this suffering . Jewish culture has always been marked by humour and story-telling. As a response to sufferings which were at times inescapable, *a type of story or humour emerged which became known as 'winning at losing'*. If you cannot escape your persecutor, you can at least solace yourself with somehow getting the better of him. Here are some examples.

"A Jew was drowning in the River Dneiper. He cried for help; at which two Czarist policeman ran up. When they saw it was a Jew they said "Let the Jew drown." When the man sensed his strength was ebbing he shouted with all his might "Down with the Czar!" Hearing such seditious words the policeman plunged in, pulled him out, and arrested him!"

"A merchant from Brisk ordered a consignment of dry goods from Lodz. A week later he received the following letter: "We regret that we cannot despatch this order until full payment has been made on the previous one." The merchant sent his reply, "Please cancel the new order, I cannot wait that long.""

Finally. "A group of Nazis surrounded an elderly Berlin Jew and demanded of him,"Tell us Jew, who caused the war?" The little Jew was no fool. "The Jews", he said, and then added, "and the bicycle riders." The Nazis were puzzled. "Why the bicycle riders?" "Why the Jews?" answered the little old man."

There is a poignancy about such stories which brings out the sorrow of their sufferings, but also their irrepressible spirit through it all.

Another characteristic of Jewish people which has resulted from persecution is *a desire to get on*. Many Jews have a natural energy which leads to this, but persecution has often increased it. When they have lost almost everything through enforced emigration, it is not surprising that they will put a lot of energy into getting 'up' again. Furthermore, gaining acceptance through being productive in society is a natural desire in those who have been rejected elsewhere. Those who dislike Jews may call this being 'pushy', and no doubt there are those who are indifferent to the needs of others in their desire to get on, but the underlying reaction to persecution needs to be understood.

It is a sad fact that all this sensitivity on the part of Jews to the way that others speak of them, does not mean that Jews hesitate to speak disparagingly of Gentiles. The Hebrew word for Gentile is 'goy', and it has been used as a term of abuse. It is not excusable, but it is an understandable reaction to what they have suffered from Gentiles. Sometimes it has provoked further persecution, when Gentiles have sensed this attitude in some Jews. The only solution is for both Jews and Gentiles to be humbled before God through the Gospel.

Anti-Semitism is not a recent phenomenon, and this means that many Jews expect it to emerge again; they just hope it will not do so in their lifetime. A Jewish man I know said to me, "the only thing which is preserving the Jews from harm in Britain today is that the Blacks and Pakistanis are first in the firing line." I felt he was exaggerating, but he was very serious. He had not suffered in the Holocaust, but he could remember being called a 'Jew-boy' at school. It had bred in him a distrust of outsiders. This means that it *takes time to win the confidence of a Jewish friend*. If you are not Jewish then you are associated with people who in his eyes have a lot to live down. It may not be expressed directly to you, but he will have an inbred caution. Be patient!

A word on the State of Israel in this context. You may feel that Israeli leaders are over-cautious, and even stubborn, in their resistance to the efforts of others to bring about peace in the Middle-East. Behind the caution lies this history of persecution. Many Israelis have had first hand experience of having to leave Gentile lands because of persecution. Hence they do not take too kindly to Gentile advice on how to behave, or immediately warm to assurances of support from them. I am not justifying all that Israel does, but I am simply saying that we must view their wariness against a backdrop of thousands of years of Gentile hostility.

There have been times in Jewish history when they have felt so crushed in spirit by persecution that it has made them open to *false Messiahs and new forms of Judaism*. About 27 men are on record as having claimed to be the Messiah, and have gained some form of following. The most notorious was Shabbatai Zvi (1626-1676), who caused a great stir in Eastern Europe and the Middle-East for a while, but ended up converting to Islam when the Sultan of Turkey threatened to execute him. A new form of Judaism sprang up in the eighteenth century when life was harsh for the Jews of Poland and Russia. We have already noticed this movement, whose followers were called Chasidic Jews. It was mystical in its orientation and emphasised joy in God in every aspect of life. Initially it was frowned upon by the Jewish establishment. But it is good to remember that in the persecutions of the nineteenth and twentieth centuries, many thousands of Jews turned to Messiah Jesus; they found no hope or comfort in either Judaism or the world.

What is the Jewish view of all this suffering? There is not a univerally accepted one. Some try to ignore it and just get on with life in the hope that it will not happen again. Many simply do not know what to make of it; it is a fact of Jewish history and they just accept it. If God is brought into the question, such people will usually shrug their shoulders. They cannot just give up believing in Him, but neither do they want to think too deeply about the questions raised by their sufferings. It is too difficult or disturbing. Some have indeed abandoned all belief in God because of their sufferings; they explain them as just another instance of man's inhumanity to man. The traditional religious response is summarised in these words from the Day of Atonement Service, "Because we transgressed, and were cast out, and our fatness turned to leanness..." The ultimate reason for Jewish national suffering is understood to be God's judgement upon Israel's sin. If you ask, what sin? the answer will not be in terms of present-day sinfulness, but rather in terms of national sin committed in the land of Israel prior to the destruction of the Temple. As Lord Jakobovits wrote in 1987 when he was the British Chief Rabbi, "the doctrine of collective reward and punishment is invariably restricted to the Jewish national experience in the land of

Israel only." What sin in the land of Israel? The one usually referred to is the hatred that existed among the various Jewish factions at the time of the fall of the Temple. They would not accept what Messiah Himself said, that it was "because you did not know the time of your visitation"(Luke 19v44).

If we take an overall view of the Jews and persecution we undoubtedly see Satan's malice, but we also see God's sovereign hand. In Appendix 3 I have made suggestions on how to deal with questions about their sufferings. At this point we should note that it has had the effect of keeping the Jews together, and that God has never allowed it to reach a point where their national survival has been threatened. He surely has a saving purpose, which will be to the glory of His name.

13.
The Jews and Christianity

The relationship between the Jews and Christianity has several aspects, but inevitably the one which colours most people's thinking is the persecution of Jews in the name of Jesus. You may be wondering why I have made no reference to this in what I have written above on the Jews and persecution. I believe it must be dealt with in a separate chapter, so as to help you to take full account of its effect upon the Jews. Perhaps nothing causes greater problems to a Christian who starts to witness to a Jewish friend than this fact of history.

One effect it has is to *reinforce the feeling that Jesus is not for the Jews.* Not only do they not want to believe in Him if that is what His followers do, but it appears that Christianity does not really want them either. Christianity is therefore seen as an enemy. Hence *to convert is a betrayal,* a going over to the enemy. One Jewish Christian author relates how the word 'betrayed' was the first word which came into his head when his daughter announced her faith in Jesus. This is why some Jewish families will go as far as cutting off anyone who believes in Jesus, although fewer Jews would do that nowadays. All this means there is *an obligation not to convert.* It is not just a matter of pressure not to believe, but most Jews are taught that it is a part of their identifying with their own that they do not believe in Jesus. A Jewish individual may sink very low; he or she may become an atheist, a bank robber, a tramp, or an army deserter, but in the eyes of Jewish relatives all of these things would be preferable to becoming a Christian. Religious Jews obviously feel these things more strongly, but there are few Jews who do not feel them at all. It is only among those younger Jews who are irreligious and materialistic that there is a greater degree of indifference to Jews who believe in Jesus.

How does a Christian respond to all this? He is obviously going to have to be very patient. He must *draw the distinction between true and false Christians,* remembering that it is not a distinction which Jews themselves make. For them there are just good and bad Christians, because all those born in a 'Christian' country are born Christian, unless they are Buddhist, Hindu, or Muslim. I am not saying that true Christians have never manifested anti-Semitic attitudes, but true faith surely cannot lead to incitement to violence against Jews. It must be firmly pointed out to them that according to the New Testament such people as the Crusaders and the Nazis cannot be Christians. You may have to say this time and again.

A further response must be to *express genuine sorrow that such things were done in the name of Jesus.* It must surely appal any Christian that this has happened. But is that enough? What of the need for repentance? If you have personally been guilty of anti-Semitic attitudes it may be appropriate to express sorrow for this, but you cannot repent of the sins of others. Some feel they ought to do this because these evil things have been done in the name of Christ, and so they somehow feel tainted with the guilt of it. But that is not Biblical; we are each responsible for our own sins. We would not accuse Jews today of being guilty of what some Jews did in opposing Jesus years ago, nor would we expect them to repent of it. Similarly we cannot repent of what others have done in Jesus' name. Even so, we must feel deeply saddened by it, and make that plain to our Jewish friends.

Ultimately this hurdle of persecution in the name of Jesus can never be overcome until Jewish people are more concerned about the hurdle of their sins. When they come to faith in Christ they will understand the difference between true and false Christians, and so be able to gain a different understanding of their history, but do not expect that to come quickly.

It is worth noting that there is an element of deliberate misinformation here. Some Jews are well aware that there are countries where Christianity has dominated national thinking, especially since the Reformation, but the Jews living there have not been persecuted. The United States is an obvious example, but it is also generally true of Canada, Great Britain, Holland, Sweden, Norway,

Switzerland, South Africa, Australia, and New Zealand. In fact it was to these 'Christian' countries that the Jews fled when they were persecuted elsewhere. Why, if Christianity always promotes anti-Semitism?

Jewish people have recognised with their feet, so to speak, that there is a true expression of Christianity which does not foster anti-Semitic attitudes. That is Protestantism, with its stress on the Scriptures. The principles of religious and political freedom which grew out of it in the Puritan era in England and America being particularly beneficial to the Jews. Stephen Brook acknowledges this in his book about the Jews in Britain called 'The Club'. He writes 'With the establishment of the Commonwealth, an opportunity arose to argue to the puritanical masters of Britain on strictly Biblical grounds that the Jews should be readmitted.' They were. He acknowledges that it was the willingness to submit to Scripture which changed things for the Jews. Chaim Raphael goes further by acknowledging in his book 'Encounters with the Jewish People' that Protestantism actually creates a culture in which Jews feel at home - 'They (Jewish immigrants) saw Protestant America as a blessed relief from the inquisitions of the past and reached out hungrily toward its culture.'

As well as all this it is often ignored that when Jews have been persecuted in the name of Jesus, true Christians have also come under attack from the same quarter. The Inquisition, for example, began by persecuting Jews, but it turned its attention to Protestants a few decades later. It is both sad and wrong that these facts are not emphasised more. It suits the Jewish leadership to draw attention to the persecutions and the sufferings, so as to keep their people together, and away from Christianity.

All this can lead to a particular problem for young Jewish believers, especially those in Israel. They sometimes find it difficult to identify with the history of the Church, as being in any way a spiritual history of which they are now a part. For years they have been taught to see it as an enemy, and that is difficult to change overnight. In some instances of course we would not wish their attitude to change. There is much in Church history, some of which is perpetuated within Christendom today, from which true Christians disassociate. However, for some Jewish believers the whole of Church history is viewed as an enemy to begin with.

Help can be given in two ways. First of all they should be introduced to the record of the true churches, and the writings of godly men of the past. As they gain personal spiritual benefit from this, they will begin to feel their spiritual oneness with true believers in all times and all places. Further to this they will need guidance on how to steer clear of the manifestations of apostasy within Christendom.

Another aspect of this relationship between the Jews and Christianity is that for centuries Christianity has been the dominant or national religion of many countries in the Western world. Jews have therefore come to view it as a Gentile religion. Consequently Jewish people brought up in such places equate being a Christian with being a Gentile. I knew a lady who once descibed a pork chop as 'Christian meat'! To her there was no distinction between Christian and Gentile. A consequence of this thinking is that *if a Jew becomes a Christian it is thought that he has become a Gentile.* Or to put it in a way in which Jewish people more frequently express it, he is no longer a Jew. An expression very common among Jews when challenged to believe in Jesus is 'I was born a Jew, I'll die a Jew!' Now that may seem obvious to you. How can a Jew cease being Jewish? But for him it is simply a way of saying he cannot possibly become a Christian, because it is the same as asking him to become a Gentile. Impossible!

I have made the point that Jewish people do not easily distinguish between true and false Christians. This leads us to another aspect of the Jews and Christianity; how the Jews view the different churches. As Jewish people look at the vast array of different churches, such as Coptic, Eastern Orthodox, Roman Catholic, and Protestant, they do not make much of a distinction between them. *They see all churches as Christian.* True Protestants may have no time for the Pope's claims to be the head of Christendom, but unfortunately Jewish people will listen to him as if he is. He has the majority of followers, and that decides the issue. I was introduced to a Jewish lady who had come to believe that Jesus is the Messiah simply by reading the Bible on her own. She then wondered which church to go to. She decided on a nearby Roman Catholic one because it was, as she thought, part of the oldest and largest Church grouping.

This tendency to see Roman Catholicism as the main expression of Christianity means that *Christianity is viewed as an inferior religion to Judaism.* That may surprise you, but you need to be aware of it. One of the reasons for this is that the Jews have learnt to avoid idolatry. The Babylonian captivity had the effect of purging idolatry out of Israel once and for all, so when Jews see idolatry in a church they react against it and see it is a sign of a departure from the commands of God. Roman Catholicism is certainly guilty at this point.

The fact that Judaism was the mother religion further enables Jews to think of Christianity as inferior; an error-tainted breakaway. Jews will agree that, for Gentiles, Christianity is an improvement on paganism, but it is not for them. This is complicated by the fact that even some true doctrines are misunderstood, and viewed as a peversion of Old Testament teaching. For instance the doctrine of the Trinity is often thought to teach a belief in three Gods, which is an abominable idea to Jews (and Christians), and definitely casts Christianity in an inferior light. The behaviour of some Churches towards the Jews has only confirmed this impression of inferiority

One final point I would make here is the effect made on Jewish people by asceticism and self-denial in Christian history. Judaism tends to stress enjoying life as a gift from God. This is illustrated by a saying in the Talmud, 'On Judgement Day a man will have to give an account for every good thing which his eye saw and he did not enjoy.' In contrast to this *Christianity is perceived as a religion of restraint.* There is truth and error here of course. True Christians would also stress enjoying life as a gift from God, and they would deny that morbid and erroneous approach to salvation which leads to monasticism. However they also recognise the power of sin, and are therefore careful in their enjoyments not to lay themselves open to temptation. The Jewish tendency is to underestimate sin and its power, and this leads Jewish people to be less cautious at this point.

With all these tensions between the Jews and Christianity will anyone be saved? Yes! Many have been and are being now. Many Jews were saved in the nineteenth century while actually fleeing from persecution by so-called Christians, having only seen corrupt forms of Christianity. As Jesus said 'All that the Father gives to me will come to me'(John 6v37). I am making you aware of these problems to encourage you to be sensitive and patient, but as you faithfully present the truth in love, you can be sure that God is well able to overcome all the obstacles, and save souls as He wills.

14.
The Jews and the Jews

I was quite amazed to see the words 'Mixed Marriages' on the front cover of an important Jewish magazine. I never imagined that they would write an article on marriages between Jews and Gentiles, because I could not think that the writer would have anything good to say. A quick glance at the article showed me I had got it all wrong. The photograph on the first page showed a handsome young couple, with the husband looking very oriental. The 'mixed' marriage was one between Jews, but those of different cultural traditions, the one Ashkenazi and the other Sephardi. The article went on to show how, contrary to the expectations of many, such marriages were working well. Does this surprise you? You have maybe thought that the Jews are the Jews, and that any differences among them could not be so large as to create such problems. They certainly can! The explanation of the differences lies in Jewish history. I want to mention some of them here and give you some information that will help you to witness sensitively. Of course there are the other more usual differences, such as rich and poor, but those are obvious and you should know how to adjust your witness to suit.

Ashkenazi Jews are those who have been brought up in a culture which developed in Europe, particularly northern Europe. The culture of *Sephardi Jews* was one which initially developed in the Mediterranean areas ruled by Islam, Spain being the main centre. There is also another cultural group, that of *the Oriental Jews* who have lived for centuries in the lands to the east of Israel. The differences between them arose due to the development of their own separate customs, and from picking up various habits and cultural traditions from their neighbours. This would include such things as dress, language, art, food, music, and even mannerisms of religious devotion. For instance when an older Ashkenazi Jew asks if you speak 'Jewish', he does not mean do you speak Hebrew. He is referring to Yiddish, a mixture of German and Hebrew written in Hebrew script. To him it is 'Jewish', but it would not be to a Sephardi, and especially not to an Oriental who speaks Tati, which is Persian written in Hebrew script! Likewise at Passover, an Ashkenazi looks forward to gefilte fish and matzah ball soup as two of the courses, but a Sephardi enjoys a more oriental preparation of fish, and cakes made of matzah meal flavoured with orange blossom and white wine. Thinking back to that article on mixed marriages I mentioned you can see the potential for discord, especially when the way to a man's heart is his stomach!

Of course in mentioning these cultural differences you must not forget that the great things which are at the core of Jewishness are held in common and bind them together. These include such things as their history, basic religious traditions, Synagogue worship, experiences of anti-Semitism, and writings such as the Talmud. Their rejection of Jesus is also a uniting factor, except, of course, for those Jews who have come to trust in Him. Such believers will share these common historical, cultural and religious influences. Some of these keep them bound to their people for ever, others cannot consistently be retained along with their faith in Jesus the Messiah.

In western countries you will rarely, if ever, meet Oriental Jews. There are Sephardi Jews in the West, especially France, but those of an Ashkenazi background are by far the majority. With the Ashkenazi Jews you will meet all the difficulties due to that 'Christian' persecution which I have been mentioning. However this is not so pronounced with Sephardi Jews, especially those who have themselves lived most of their lives in Muslim lands. They have not experienced this persecution at first hand, and so are usually more open to listen to the Gospel. I remember speaking to a devout Persian-born Jewish man after an open-air meeting in London. He was discussing matters in a very unprejudiced way, and was fascinated when he was shown certain Messianic prophecies. He had never heard of such things and was genuinely inquisitive. An orthodox Ashkenazi lady was nearby, and took it upon herself to intervene and try to stir up prejudice against Jesus. But he told her to go away, and in no uncertain terms! All this makes Jewish witness very interesting! It also underlines the need to listen to your Jewish friend; the basic need of all Jews is the same, but there are many differences to which we need to be sensitive.

What about the situation in Israel, and that of Israelis you might meet outside of Israel? There are Jews from all these different backgrounds in Israel. When Jews began returning to Palestine in large numbers most of them were from Ashkenazi stock. It was not until after 1948 that many Sephardi Jews began to come to Israel because of having to leave Arab lands. Today the Sephardi Jews are in the majority.

'Sabras' are those Jews born and brought up in Israel. These tend to be more open to the Gospel, except the more orthodox ones, because they have not been brought up in Christendom. However, it does not help that they are surrounded by a vast array of Christian 'holy' sites, most of which bring the Gospel into disrepute. What does help them to be more open is that Jesus once lived there too. He is not so easily brushed aside as a foreign influence. This is underlined by the impact being made by the growing number of local congregations in the land. However it should not be assumed from this that Israelis are unaffected by the history of persecution in the name of Jesus. That part of their history is taught in the schools of Israel, and they are prejudiced by it.

A final factor which I want to mention is that Israel is a secular State. Its founders were non-religious and they would not have the word 'God' in the Constitution. Israel began with humanistic ideals but they are now generally admitted to have failed. Wars, and the need to be ready for war, has hardened the feelings of many Israeli Jews in a way that few of them would have imagined possible. The need to keep down Arab unrest has cast them in the mould of oppressors, something which has shaken many to the core. It is all a far cry from the moral example to the nations they were hoping to be. There is a spiritual vacuum in the soul of the nation which more and more of its people are feeling. This is leading to all sorts of ideas for a cure, including an interest in orthodox Judaism, but we can thank God that an increasing number are coming to faith in Jesus the Messiah. He is the one who can be presented to Israeli Jews as one of their own, and their only hope.

15.
The Jews and Israel today

If you are familiar with cricket you will know what I mean when I say that for many Jews, Israel is a 'long stop'. He is the fielder behind the wicket-keeper in schoolboy cricket who you hope will never be needed, but is there just in case both batsman and wicket-keeper miss the ball! Most Jews are glad that Israel is there. If persecution should rear its head again it is good to know that there is one place of refuge on the earth where they will be guaranteed immediate access. Even so, most have no intention of going to live there, and hope that they will never have to. As one Jewish young man put it, 'One of the golden rules of Anglo-Jewry is 'Visit Israel, but don't stay there.''

Your Jewish friend is likely to be in this category, but do not assume that he has no special feelings towards Israel. It is not only a long stop - Israel has given the Jews something to be proud of on the world stage. For centuries the Jews have been 'guests' in the lands of others and wherever they have gone their achievements have been significant, but they have always been reluctant to herald them too strongly to non-Jews. The reason for this is that they have been wary of stirring up envy, or of underlining their Jewishness and so drawing attention to the fact that they are 'outsiders'. But Israel is different. She is obviously Jewish – homegrown, so to speak – and a clear evidence of what the Jews can do if they are given a free hand. And they have done a great deal. Israeli achievements in settlement, agriculture, economic development, defence, education, and health care are considerable.

Early settlements, like the Kibbutzim, demonstrated the tremendous willingness of the people to work together for a common goal. The development of the land from arid wastes, rock strewn hillsides, and malaria-infested swamps to vast tracts of arable land, has led to Israel being mostly self-sufficent, and indeed an exporter of many foodstuffs. The agricultural techniques she has developed have benefitted other nations. Her educational system provides state-funded teaching up to University level, and there are many overseas students who come to benefit from her institutions. She has developed a network of surgeries and hospitals for health care. Despite an enormous defence budget, few natural resources, and a workforce which needed much retraining, the Israeli economy grew rapidly in its first 25 years due to imaginative enterprise and sheer hard work. Israel would rather that her defence forces were not so famous, but the need to survive against hostile neighbours has meant the development of highly effective military units which have successfully defended the country against numerically superior forces on several occasions. Here are many things to admire and it is good to be ready to do so when Israel is mentioned.

You may be thinking to yourself that this is all very well, but not all in the garden is rosy in Israel today. Very true, criticisms of her treatment of her Arab citizens and of her weakness at curbing the undemocratic measures of her Orthodox politicians are justified. But let me stress to you the need to be positive first of all. That is the Lord's way with us, and it should be our way with others. World opinion is moving against Israel, and the western media are often very negative in their attitude. People are forgetful of Israel's past history and her present achievements. Jews everywhere feel threatened by this, and are very grateful of any expression of support from Gentiles. Here is an opportunity for Christians to show a genuine concern for Israel's welfare.

Bearing all this in mind, you may be surprised to find that your Jewish friend is very critical of Israel. He may do no more than express that common alarm which we all feel when we see injustice or dishonesty. However his criticisms could be inspired by something more. Jewishness forms a bond between Israelis and the Jews elsewhere, and if Israel behaves badly then it reflects on them all. Bad behaviour by Israel stirs up anti-Semitism elsewhere. That is of obvious concern to your Jewish friend!

Therefore he feels torn. When it comes to the bottom line he will support Israel, but if he does not criticise her failures he will appear immoral. And yet if he does that too strongly in public he will encourage anti-Semitism. He would agree with what G.K.Chesterton once said to a hostile reporter, 'I don't criticise my friends to my enemies.' The practical point is this, if you hear your friend express such criticisms of Israel be careful how you agree with him. If you join in with his criticism of Israel be careful not to create the impression that you are insensitive to his fears for her wellbeing. On a human level Israel emerged because of Gentile persecution of the Jews, and it is still a 'long stop' today, so your friend must know that you appreciate this if you are going to express criticism. Otherwise he may be less trustful of you, and therefore less open to hear the Gospel from you.

I have written about this at some length because Israel is frequently in the news, and many Jews that you meet will be interested to discuss the issues with you. Your attitude will be important to them. Gentile friends of Israel are highly regarded by the Jews, and if you express a genuine sympathy and concern it will win confidence, and probably a willingness to hear the Gospel from you.

What about modern Israel as a fulfilment of prophecy? For their part, Jewish people have returned to the land as an escape from troubles elsewhere, but do they see the hand of God in it all as predicted in the Scriptures? As a matter of fact, not many do. I knew a young man in Brighton whose job it was to encourage his fellow Jews in Britain to emigrate to Israel (to make Aliyah), but he was totally ignorant of the Biblical passages which pointed to this return! Now, I have not written this book to discuss the subject of prophecy, and I am aware that Christians do not agree on the interpretation of the various passages. But for those who are convinced that these things were predicted (for those who are not convinced I have listed a few references in Appendix 2) I want to say something on their use in witnessing.

God's ultimate end in bringing the Jews back to the land is clearly stated in Ezekiel 39v26-29, 'after they have borne their shame, and all their unfaithfulness.....then they shall know that I am the LORD their God, who sent them into captivity among the nations, but also brought them back to their own land, and left none of them captive any longer....' God's purpose is to humble them before Him and then to save them. This means that prophecy should not be used in such a way that it will boost Israel's pride. Rather it should be used to show them their sinfulness and God's great mercy to them. This will lead on naturally to presenting the Gospel. Another approach is to use prophecy to establish the authority and reliability of the Scriptures by pointing out how the prophets of Israel, Messiah Jesus, and His Apostles, spoke of the exile and the return. From there you can go on to show the Biblical teaching concerning individual salvation, through Jesus' fulfilment of the Messianic prophecies.

That last sentence raises the obvious question 'how do I do that?' The chapters which now follow go into more detail about communicating the Gospel to Jewish people, and leading them to a personal faith in the Lord Jesus. So far I have concentrated on helping you to 'sit where they sit', but the time comes when we have to speak out the truth. What follows gives some guidance on that.

16.
The Messenger, the message and messianic fulfilment

The Messenger

A messenger! Is that how you think of yourself when you speak to others of Christ? It may not be the full picture but it emphasises something important, we are handing on what has been said by God, not our own ideas. When Billy Graham preaches he has a habit of holding up his Bible to make it as visible as possible; he is making this same point. Our hearers must realise that we are only saying what God has already said, and we can only use the Bible to make that plain. And we must use it.

We are more than messengers though. A messenger is not a person with authority, yet we are. The One who said, "All authority has been given to me in heaven and on earth"(Matthew 28v28), has commanded us to take the message out. For this reason Paul calls himself an ambassador for Christ (2Cor 5v20), one who comes with the fulness of Christ's authority and speaking only His message.

As well as this we are witnesses. That is, we are people with a personal involvement in the message. We are witnesses to the truth of God's Word because we have believed its promises and not been disappointed. We are witnesses to God in our lives through Jesus Christ in that He has forgiven our sins and we know Him. We are also witnesses in a secondary sense, in that we hand on the eye-witness accounts of those who saw and heard Jesus the Messiah.

This does not mean that we force ourselves on people in a fever of human excitement or psychological compulsion. But these definitions of our role should save us from two pitfalls in evangelism.

Firstly, an awareness that we are messengers will help us to avoid the danger of drawing attention to ourselves. Secondly, knowing that we are ambassadors and witnesses will preserve us from the weakness of speaking as if we are mere traders in ideas, engaging only in abstract discussion, or simply suggesting a better way.

The Message

This section contains many references to Bible verses, which for convenience are listed at the end. I would suggest that you read straight through the section first of all, without stopping to look them up. Afterwards you can return to study those texts, and similar ones, to help you in your personal witness.

Jesus' own words in Mark 1v15 are the best summary of our message that we can find, "The time is fulfilled, and the kingdom of God is at hand. Repent, and believe the gospel." It puts the Gospel in its proper setting, and then it speaks of God, our sin, and God's good news of salvation; finally it demands a response.

"The time is fulfilled"
What time? Jesus was speaking to His own people, the Jews; a people who were conscious of God's promises to save and deliver them. To different degrees they were waiting for this, although they obviously had different ideas about what form it would take. Jesus is saying, 'the deliverance is here!' When speaking to Jews you are speaking to people with a similar consciousness, and so in declaring the message you should aim to begin with the Hebrew Scriptures. You must make it plain that all you are saying was promised to Israel.

Does this mean that as you speak to a Jewish friend you immediately plunge into a whole string of Messianic prophecies with the aim of proving that Jesus is the Messiah? Well, no. It is possible to convince Jewish people that Jesus is the Messiah in that way, and yet it may be no more than a mental assent. This can happen if prophecy is used as a battering ram to pressurise them into an intellectual submission. The proper function of such prophecies is to use them as a part of your presentation of the overall message of the Scriptures on God, man, and the way of salvation. The following is a brief summary of that message constructed around Jesus' words in Mark 1v15.

"God"

God is holy, He is high and lifted up,[1] and unless He reveals Himself to us we are left ignorant.[2] He made the whole universe by His great power,[3] and to this day it displays His great wisdom and might.[4] In it He placed man, making him in His own image, to glorify and enjoy Him.[5] How great He is! And we must speak of Him as the One who truly is great. The Gospel starts with God, indeed it is "the gospel of God"(Romans 1v1), and although you should not be wooden and imagine your witness must always literally start there, yet that is its setting. What we have to say about sin and the Saviour will lose their force unless God's holiness and greatness are conveyed, along with His wrath against sinners. Jews who are ignorant of the Scriptures do not know what He is really like, so do not assume that they have a correct concept of God. Even the more devout Jews lack a proper intellectual understanding of what God is like, because so much of their thinking is based on tradition and not Scripture. Teaching them about God is part of your message.

"The kingdom of God"

This is not so much a place as a people; it is the people whom God rules and who submit to His kingship. In that sense its beginnings were with Adam and Eve in the Garden, but they rebelled against His rule. However, God swiftly announced His determination to establish a people who would submit to Him,[6] and this set purpose of the LORD is often restated in Scripture.[7] The establishment of Israel as God's kingdom people was a major step in this purpose,[8] but its fulness awaited the coming of the Messiah.[9] This is what Jesus announced as now "at hand", which means that it was no longer out of reach, but could be entered there and then. Through Jesus the Messiah, God began to be earnestly engaged in bringing men and women, Jews and Gentiles, back under His rule and blessing. All who submit to Jesus the Messiah are in the Kingdom of God, and they alone.[10] He is continuing that purpose to this day, and you are His servant to urge others to come back to God their maker. What a privilege! What a responsibility!

Man in sin
Jesus' words in Mark assume this, without specifically mentioning it. When Adam sinned all humanity fell with him,[11] and that includes Jewish people.[12]. Sin can be described as rebellion against God's rule, and one consequence for man has been an ignorance of what God requires.[13] But it is worse than that, because there is also an unwillingness to listen when he is told.[14] Man then goes on to deceive himself that all is really OK.[15] Man is dead spiritually.[16] He is a sinner, and he sins because of it.[17] Man is not born into God's kingdom, he is not naturally among those who love God and submit to Him, rather he is a stooge of Satan.[18] If he is to get into God's kingdom he is entirely dependant on God deciding to be gracious to him.[19] In practice Jewish people hardly believe any of this. Of course they believe they are sinners, but they do not grasp the hopelessness of their position. You have to make that plain.

"The Gospel"
Good news! God has done something to redeem a hopeless situation, to bring multitudes of rebels back to Himself. Because of this they can have their guilt removed, receive forgiveness of their sins, and be restored to fellowship with Him. In all this He has taken the initiative[20] and He will surely complete His purpose.[21] It is all inspired by God's love for His lost creatures,[22] and it is based on the atoning work of Jesus the Saviour.[23] The sentence of God's law on the sinner is death, which involves everlasting punishment,[24] but God made it plain to Israel that He would accept the death of a substitute and so forgive the sinner.[25] He then clearly predicted that the Messiah would be the substitute who would make a true atonement.[26] God took this great step because man is totally incapable of atoning for his own sin.[27] Therefore God Himself promised to come among men to save them.[28] A man in ancient Greece who taught his pupils the art of writing plays once said to them, "Don't bring a god on to the stage unless you really have to." That is true in God's plan of salvation; He came because there was no other way.[29]

And He did come! The second Person of the Godhead, the Son of God, took human nature[30] and achieved all this by dying as a substitute on the cross,[31] bearing God's wrath against rebel sinners,[32] and then being raised from the dead because death could not hold

Him.[33] God promised all this to the Jews, and it is now a part of history, Jewish history. They of all people should believe it!

"Repent and believe"

The word repent underlines that man is not a neutral moral being. He is a rebel. In Jesus' day the nation of Israel was God's kingdom, but that did not remove the need for them to make a personal response to God; Jesus clearly required it. He does today. Repentance is essentially a change of mind, which is intimately connected to a change of attitude of heart.[34] It involves a person recognising that they have sinned against God, and that they deserve His judgement. It means that they are sorry for their sin, and confess it to God,[35] determining that they will from that moment follow Him.[36] However, this is not enough on its own, although many Jews believe that it is. They even believe their repentance atones for sin, especially on the Day of Atonement. But Moses never taught that, and Jesus the Messiah calls for more. He commands belief.

There must be a belief, a trust, in God's provision of atonement for sin in the death of Jesus.[37] Belief in Him is a confession that we cannot atone for our own sins, but that we can hope for forgiveness only in Jesus the Messiah, God's suffering Servant. Belief involves a trust in Christ Himself.[38] It is not simply believing certain things about Him, although that is vital, it is putting our personal trust in a living person who died for sinners. Whatever obstacles the experiences of Jewish history have put in the way of Jews coming to this faith, it cannot be sidestepped. He alone died for sinners.[39]

"The kingdom of God"(again)

A Jewish person who repents and believes is, by God's grace, in the kingdom of God. Jesus the Messiah is the ruler of that kingdom,[40] and they are to follow Him as He guides them into a true submission to God.[41] Jesus does not want adherents, but disciples; those who out of love for Him will follow Him as their true Shepherd and King.[42] His Spirit has worked the miracle of the new birth to make them desire all this,[43] and He also gives the power to do it.[44] God's Word guides them into what He wants.[45] In chapter 20 I will go into more detail about the particular help which a new Jewish believer needs to be able to grow as a member of God's kingdom.

Scripture verses on The Message
These verses demonstrate the points made in the section above.

Ref.	Old Testament text	New Testament text	NT quote of OT
1	Lev. 19v2; Isa. 6v1-3	Rev. 15v4	1 Pet. 1v16
2	Job 36v26; Isa. 55v8,9	Eph. 4v17,18	Rom. 11v34
3	Gen. 1v31-2v1; Psa. 95v5	Rev. 4v11	1 Cor. 10v26
4	Ps. 19v1-4	Rom. 1v19,20	Rom. 10v18
5	Gen. 5v1,2; Psa. 73v25,26	John 10v10; I Cor. 10v31	
6	Gen. 3v15		
7	Num. 14v21; Habb. 2v14		
8	Ex. 19 v5,6		
9	Dan. 7v13,14		
10	Joel 2v32	Col. 1v13,14	Rom. 10v13
11	Gen. 5v3	1 Cor. 15v21,22	
12	Rom. 3v23		
13	Job 37v19; Prov. 4v19	Eph. 4v18; 1 Pet. 2v9	Matt. 4v16
14	Gen. 8v21	Rom. 8v7; 1 Cor. 2v14	Rom. 3v10-18
15	Jer. 17v9	Jas. 1v22; 1 John 1v8	
16	Gen. 2v17, 3v24	Eph. 2v1	
17	Deut. 32v5,6; Psa. 14v1-3	Matt. 12v33,34; John 8v34	
18	Deut. 32v17	2 Tim. 2v26	
19	Deut. 32v39; Isa 45v22-25	Eph. 2v8; 1 John 5v12	
20	Deut. 4v37; Isa. 64v4	Eph. 1v4; 1 John 4v19	1 Cor. 2v9
21	Isa. 9v7	John 10v28	
22	Ex. 34v6,7; Lam. 3v22	John 3v16	
23	Isa. 53v10	Lk. 24v46,47	
24	Gen. 2v17; Ez. 18v4	Rom. 6v23; Matt. 25v46	Gal. 3v10
25	Ex. 12v13; Lev. 16v15-17, 17v11		
26	Isa. 52v13-53v12	Mk. 10v45	
27	Psa. 49v5-9; Isa. 64v6	Mk. 8v37; Lk. 18v9-14	
28	Isa. 7v14, 9v6; Jer. 23v5,6	Matt. 1v23; Heb. 1v5	Matt. 1v23
29	Hos. 13v9,14	Gal. 3v21,22	
30		John 1v14,18; Rom. 8v3	
31	Psa. 22v14-18	Lk. 23v46; 1 Pet. 2v24	
32	Isa. 53v6	1 John 2v2	
33	Psa. 16v10; Isa. 53v10	Lk. 24v6,7; Acts 2v24	Acts 2v25-31
34	Deut. 30v2; Hos. 14v1-3	2 Cor. 7v9-11	
35	Ex. 33v1-6; 2 Chr. 6v28-30	Acts 2v37,38; 1 John 1v9	
36	Deut. 4v39,40; Hos. 6v1-3	Matt. 3v7,8; Titus 3v8	
37	Isa. 53v1	Rom. 3v25	Rom. 10v16
38		John 11v25,26	
39		Acts 4v12; Rom. 5v6-8	

Ref.	Old Testament text	New Testament text
40		Matt. 28v18; Col. 1v13
41	Deut. 18v15-19	Matt. 5-7; John 17v26
42		Mk. 8v34-38, John 8v30-32
43	Ezek. 36v26,27;Isa. 59v21	John 3v3,5
44	Isa. 44v1-5	Rom. 8v13; Gal. 5v16
45	Psa. 119v9,105	John 17v17

Messianic Fulfilment

Let me begin by repeating what I said earlier: Messianic prophecies must be used as a coherent part of presenting the Gospel message. They should not be quoted in a random fashion as if the recognition of their remarkable fulfilment will, in itself, convert souls. And they should never be used as missiles to be fired at an opponent in a war of words. Of course, the fulfilment of prophecy is an important factor in demonstrating the truthfulness of the message, but it should be considered in the context of the message itself. How best to use particular prophecies to this end will obviously depend on the conversation you are involved in. Once you are familiar with the prophecies, you must then trust the Holy Spirit to guide you.

A word about the style of Old Testament prophecy. Interpreting it is not always as straightforward as it seems, and what appears perfectly obvious to you may not be so to your Jewish friend. At the end of this section is a list of the most significant Messianic predictions, and most of them are what I will call direct prophecies. That is, it is clear from the context and language that the prophet is speaking of another person, who is the Messiah. However this is not always obvious to the less religious Jews, who do not dwell in the thought-world of the people of the Bible. This is particularly true of the earlier prophecies, which are either words of God Himself, or uttered by those who are not normally viewed as prophets. For example in Genesis 22v18 the words "In your seed shall all the nations of the earth be blessed because you have obeyed my voice" may not be immediately understood as Messianic because your friend has lost all sense of the need for a special deliverer. For the patriarchs and the faithful in Israel, who were so aware of that need, these words pointed to the expected deliverer being one of Abraham's descendants; and they rejoiced in it. The later prophecies, which develop these earlier themes of the promised deliverer, and which provide far more detail and colour, underline that these earlier predictions did indeed refer to the Messiah.

The other point to bear in mind is that some prophecies are the writer's account of his own experience, or that of the nation, and as such they do not immediately appear to relate to the Messiah. They are predictions because the New Testament quotes the prophecy as Messianic, and because the one in view in the account is a type of Christ, one who according to the New Testament foreshadows Messiah's ministry. An obvious example is Psalm 22. David wrote it of his own experience, but it was prophetic without his fully realising it. There are two perspectives from which we can view what was happening with this prophecy. Firstly, as the Messiah is descended from David, and it was predicted that He too would be the king of Israel, we would expect some of David's experiences to mirror those of the Messiah. Hence Jesus frequently took David's words and used them to express His own feelings. For example His use of the words of Psalm 22v1 "My God, my God, why have you forsaken me" at His crucifixion. Secondly, we can see Christ prior to His incarnation speaking through David in the words of the Psalm. Hebrews 2v12 justifies this approach; "Jesus is not ashamed to call them brothers. He says, 'I will declare your name to my brothers..'", which are the words of v22 in Psalm 22. Both perspectives are valid, but when reasoning with a Jewish friend the first will be the easier to grasp to begin with.

The Servant Songs of Isaiah are another, though different, example. The nation of Israel is God's servant, and many of these servant predictions in Isaiah can refer to it. Acts 13v47 is a New Testament example of such a usage. But in Isaiah 49v3 the word Israel is used to describe an individual, the Servant Messiah, and in Isaiah 53v8 the Servant is an individual distinct from the nation itself. Clearly these servant prophecies find their ultimate fulfilment in the ministry of the Messiah, who performs the service perfectly.

The list of prophecies below are, in the main, given in the order in which they came to Israel, so as to give an idea of the way in which the picture of the Messiah emerged to them. This will help you to keep them in context and perspective when quoting them. They are of the direct type unless an asterisk appears beside them, where they are prediction through a type. Study them as you have time; it will be a blessing to your own soul, and it will equip you to witness to your Jewish friend of Him of whom Moses and the prophets spoke.

Theme	Old Testament	New Testament
Mankind's deliverer is born of a woman	Gen. 3v15	Gal. 4v4; Rev. 12v1-5
He will be of the seed of Abraham	Gen. 22v18	Matt. 1v1; Luke 3v34
All nations will be blessed through Him	Gen. 22v18	Rom. 15v17-19; Acts 19v18-20
He will be of the tribe of Judah	Gen. 49v10	Luke 3v33; Heb. 7v14
He will be a unique prophet, like Moses	Deut. 18v15-19	Matt 7v28,29; Jn. 6v14 Acts 3v22-26
He will be of the line of David	2Sam. 7v12,13; Psa. 89v3,4; Jer. 23v5,6	Matt 1v1; Acts 2v30-36 2 Tim. 2v8
He will be the anointed of the LORD (Messiah)	Psa. 2v2; Isa. 61v1	Jn. 1v32,33; Matt. 12v28
Messiah will not see corruption i.e. He will be resurrected	Psa. 16v10 Isa. 53v10	Acts 13v35-37 Jn. 20
Messiah is the Son of God	Psa. 2v7	Matt. 3v17; Jn. 10v36-38 Rom. 1v4
Messiah's death by crucifixion(*)	Psa. 22v14-18; Psa. 69v21	Matt. 27v34-50 Jn. 19v28-30
Messiah's ascension to heaven(*)	Psa. 68v18	Acts 1v9-11; Eph. 4v7-10
Messiah's worldwide reign	Psa. 72 Isa. 11	Begun: Matt. 28v18 Completed: Matt.24v29,30; 1 Cor.15v25-28
Messiah's rule is from heaven	Psa. 110v1	Acts 2v33-36; Heb. 1v3
Messiah to be a priest, of the order of Melchizedek	Psa. 110v4	Heb. 5v5,6
Messiah opposed and rejected by rulers	Psa. 118v22,23 Psa. 2v2,3	Matt. 26v63-66, 27v26 Matt. 21v42

Theme	Old Testament	New Testament
Opposition to Messiah by Jew and Gentile	Psa. 2v1; Psa. 110v1,2 Isa. 53v1,3	Jn. 8v48,19v2,3; Acts 14v4-7
Messiah to be conceived by a virgin	Isa. 7v14	Matt. 1v20-23 Luke 1v35
Messiah to be God with us	Isa. 7v14, Isa. 9v6,7 Psa. 45v6,7; Mic. 5v2	Jn. 1v14,8v58; Acts 20v28
Messiah's kingdom to be a growing one	Isa. 9v7; Isa. 42v3,4	Matt. 28v19; 1 Cor. 15v25,26
Galilee will be a significant area in Messiah's ministry	Isa. 9v1,2	Matt. 4v13-17
Messiah to be anointed by God's Spirit	Isa. 11v2,61v1	Mk. 1v9-11; Lk. 4v16-21; Acts 10v38
Messiah to work miracles	Isa. 35v5,6	Mk. 1v32-34
Messiah to be the Servant of the LORD	Isa. 42v1, 49v3,50v10, 52v13; Zech. 3v8	Mk. 10v45; Jn. 13v1-17
Messiah's ministry to be unpretentious	Isa. 42v2	Matt. 12v15-21
Messiah's atoning work for sinners	Isa. 52v13-53v12; Hos. 13v14; Dan. 9v24,26	The Gospel accounts. Acts 8v30-35; Lk. 24v44-48; 1 Cor. 15v3,4; 1 Pet. 2v21-24
The name "the LORD" applied to Messiah	Jer. 23v5,6	
Messiah is our righteousness	Jer. 23v5,6; Dan. 9v24	Rom. 3v22-24 1 Cor. 1v30
Messiah will come in power and in glory	Dan. 7v13,14	Matt. 26v63,64, 24v30

Theme	Old Testament	New Testament
The time of Messiah's coming	Dan. 9v24-26	Gal. 4v4
Messiah to be born in Bethlehem	Mic. 5v2	Matt. 2v1-6; Lk. 2v1-7
Messiah shall be both priest and king	Zech. 6v12,13	Heb. 10v12,13
Messiah will enter Jerusalem on a donkey	Zech. 9v9	Matt. 21v1-11
Messiah will be pierced	Zech. 12v10	Jn. 19v34,37
A special messenger, 'Elijah', will prepare Messiah's way	Mal. 3v1, 4v5; Isa. 40v3-5	Matt. 11v7-15 Lk. 3v1-6,16;
Messiah will refine God's people and turn them to righteousness	Mal. 3v2-5	Matt. 5-7

17.
Ways of reaching Jewish people with the gospel

The main aim of this book is to help you with your personal witness to Jews in day-to-day living; but what if you have a desire to reach out to Jews whom you would not expect to meet in that way? Perhaps there is a Jewish community in your own town, or even your church neighbourhood. Here are some comments and suggestions on how you might go about reaching them with the Gospel.

The Jewish community

First of all you need to realise that to live in a neighbourhood or town where there is a Jewish community does not make you a part of it. That should be obvious. Community is not primarily a matter of geography, but of family, religion, and culture. You must be born into it to really belong. If you want to evangelise the Jewish community you can either do it by entering it as a guest, or by approaching it as an outsider who has an important message to communicate.

I have used the words 'guest' and 'outsider' quite deliberately. The assumption at the back of my mind is that most of my readers are of a Gentile background. From such a background you can only approach the Jewish community as a guest or an outsider, regardless of how many Jewish neighbours you have, or how much you know about Jewish ways. For a Jewish Christian things are different; they were born into the community, and nothing can alter that. Of course, many Jews will strongly assert that Jewish Christians are no longer

Jews because they believe in Jesus, but they cannot gainsay the fact that they were brought up in their community. This means that the Jewish Christian can take a different approach at times. He can speak as an insider, even though he may not always be accepted as such. Having said all that, there is much that Christians from either a Jewish or a Gentile background will have in common in the way they witness to Jews, so I am sure that what follows will be useful to all Christians.

Evangelising as a Guest

What I mean by this is getting involved in Jewish events and activities, and taking opportunities to witness as they naturally arise. But remember, if you are a guest in someone else's home, you do not act as if you own it! You are careful to fit in with the way they do things. You are sensitive. You should be so when you enter the Jewish community. But how do you enter it? There are all sorts of activities taking part in the Jewish community in which you may be interested to take part. There are Hebrew classes, lectures on Israel, Jewish history, and current affairs; classes on Israeli dancing, Jewish cookery etc etc. These are advertised in a variety of ways, such as in the 'Jewish Chronicle' which is the Jewish national newspaper in the UK, in a local Jewish paper, at the local library, or at the Jewish community centre in your town.

You will be made welcome at such gatherings, although people will obviously be wondering why you are there. This brings me to a fundamental point; be a willing guest! Do not attend such meetings if you are not genuinely interested in their content or activities. Evangelism in this context is a strictly secondary activity, which will spring out of getting to know people in a social setting which you both enjoy. If you do not enjoy it, then do not do it. You should only carry on with such activities if you can develop an easiness with the Jewish people there. So, feel free to try making contact in this way, but if after a while you are not at ease, then do not pursue it. Do not be discouraged if this is the case for you; none of us can expect to feel at ease in every situation we encounter. There are other ways for you to express your love for the Jews and reach them with the Gospel.

What about visiting a synagogue? This can be well worthwhile. Going to a Service will give you a feel for things, but you can also look around when it is not in use. Let me say though that you should not go for the purpose of evangelism. I am sure you would not like it if some Mormons came to your services to propagate their views. You would be entitled to view it as disrespectful, and an infringement of your liberty to worship in peace. Jewish people would feel the same way. So you are going for your own education, but how do you set about it? You could ask your Jewish friend to take you to his synagogue, that would certainly be the most natural way. If that is not possible you could ring the Rabbi, expressing your interest, and asking if someone would meet you and guide you through the Service. You are of course an observer, and not a worshipper, and so you should not feel any problem at being there. However, you may be pleasantly surprised at the amount of Biblical content in the worship, although you will be saddened that people are seeking to approach the LORD regardless of the way He has revealed. It is also possible for a church group to be given a guided tour of the synagogue by the Rabbi, and this is best arranged through your Pastor. You do not get to observe a service this way, but if the Rabbi makes an effort you will learn more about Judaism. If you can both go to a service and have a tour, then so much the better.

Evangelising as a Outsider

Jewish people may not always welcome the evangelistic approaches of the local church, but they have come to expect such approaches in countries moulded by Protestantism. Whatever methods you use to reach people, if you expect to encounter Jews then you should be prepared.

How do you recognise Jewish people in your neighbourhood? As far as physical appearance is concerned Jewish people are not as recognisable as some people seem to think, but once you start to make an approach with the Gospel, most Jews will let you know that they are Jewish! Jewish homes are recognisable by the mezuzah fixed to the right hand front door post. These come in all shapes and sizes, but are generally like a small rectangular box nailed to the post.

Mezuzah

Inside this small box is a parchment scroll with the words of Deuteronomy 6v4-9 and 11v13-21 hand written upon it in Hebrew. It is a reminder to those living in the home to keep God's law. Sad to say, it is often treated in a superstitious way. However, it tells you that the people living there are Jewish.

If your church is engaged in door-to-door visitation then when you come to a Jewish home you should make a straightforward approach as a visitor from a local church. It will probably be helpful if you refer to the Mezuzah from the start to make it clear that you are aware it is a Jewish home. You can then proceed to use whatever evangelistic approach you have planned for that occasion. If you want to offer some literature, then make it plain that it is written specially for Jewish people. If you do not have any then 'Christian Witness to Israel' can supply you with some, just write to the address at the back of the book.

If your church has a regular newsletter to its neighbourhood, then you could have an occasional article for Jews in it. The theme might be connected to a Jewish Festival, or the testimony of a Jewish Christian, or something of more general Jewish interest. Whatever literature you use, make sure that Jewish people have an easy means of making an initial response; do not expect them to just come to the church.

You could arrange special meetings with topics of particular interest to Jewish people. These can be connected to specific Jewish festivals, but that is not essential, there are other subjects which can be chosen.

Most churches have a notice board outside; why not use it to wish a Happy New Year to your Jewish neighbours at the time of Rosh Hashanah? It does not mean you believe that your religions are much the same, but it makes it clear that you are aware of your Jewish neighbours, and that you wish them well.

If all this sounds too much and you feel unprepared, then 'Christian Witness to Israel' or others can organise a programme of teaching on Jewish evangelism for you. This could be linked to a period of visiting Jewish neighbours together with church members.

So you have contacted a Jewish neighbour through your evangelism, and they have been prepared to listen to you. Then what? You will probably feel it would be much better if they could come and hear God's Word preached, and also to meet other Christians, especially those with greater experience of talking with Jews. By all means invite them to one of your meetings, but it is best if that does not involve coming to the church premises to begin with. Most Jews see that as a big step. Perhaps you have a Home Meeting, or a Coffee Bar; some youth activities, or a church outing. Think and pray about it, then make a warm and straightforward invitation. If at first it is refused, do not assume that is a final refusal of any further invitations. It may just take time to adjust to the idea.

One final consideration. What about sending a missionary to the Jews from your own congregation? Of course we cannot create such ourselves, but Jesus did tell us to pray to the Lord of the harvest that He would send out labourers into His harvest. Does your church do that? I hope so; and if you do then it is likely that God will call someone from among you.

Whether you are a guest or an outsider in your evangelistic approach, you will need to be ready for the ways in which Jews frequently respond to such efforts. I will give some more advice on this in Chapter 19, and also in Appendix 3 on frequent responses.

18.
Get your approach right

The time-honoured way of falling into error is to over-emphasise one truth. So far I have put before you some basic truths concerning the Jews and witnessing to them, but if you over-emphasise any one of them you will start to go wrong. Some have done this, and so I need to mention the dangers.

Some will say that my aim here is unnecessary because it is negative. If that is so, then there is a lot of unnecessary teaching in the New Testament. To faithfully teach the truth, but then to say nothing about significant deviations from it is unfaithfulness. My purpose, though, is positive – because a wrong approach in evangelism will inevitably have a damaging effect on those we lead to the Lord. For example, if an aircraft makes a wrong approach to a runway it may well land safely, but not without some uncomfortable last minute change of direction, or even some damage to the aircraft on touchdown. This is true in the spiritual realm. Evangelistic approaches which are inconsistent with the truth about the Jews and their spiritual condition are bound to have a damaging effect on new converts, even though they are truly converted. We all need to be careful, not only about the Gospel we preach, but also about the way we preach it.

There is no need

One strand of thinking within the Christian Church on the Jews holds that God has no future purposes for them as a nation. Such a view does not necessarily imply a lack of compassion for the Jews, and many who hold it have an evangelistic concern for the Jewish people. However, in earlier ages it was often associated with the idea that they were only preserved as a people as a demonstration of God's judgement. It was a short but sinful step to use this as a justification for anti-Semitism, and it often was. There are some church leaders today who are very aware of all this history, and in seeking to redress the balance they have become unscriptural in their stress on the privileged position of the Jews. They have accepted that God's covenant with Abraham and his descendants is enough to save them. Put more popularly: the Gentiles need Jesus, but the Jews are already God's children. This sometimes goes by the name of the 'Two-covenant theory'.

Such thinking will not cut much ice with anyone who has a concern to evangelise Jews. If Jesus is not the Messiah of the Jews, He is no one's Messiah! For them the Bible's message of reconciliation with God only through the death of Jesus, the Mediator of the New Covenant, is final. It was undoubtedly a great privilege to be a part of God's earlier covenants, but there was nothing in them to save from His wrath, they were preparatory to Messiah's work under the New Covenant. Under those covenants God was being forbearing with sin, not actually punishing it (Romans 3v25). That is not to say that none were saved under those earlier covenants; clearly many were, but it was on the basis of the future work of the Messiah.

However, the danger is that such 'two-covenant' thinking will cut a groove in the ice. By which I mean it may cause us to feel less urgent about their need to hear and believe the Gospel. His past dealings with them might lead some to think their situation is not quite so desperate as that of others. His promises to them for the future, especially when it is believed the fulfilment is imminent, may lead to a complacency. But none of those privileges will save them, and we must work urgently for their salvation now

Love

The sufferings of the Jews at the hands of so-called Christians is a fact that stares us in the face. The danger is that we can emphasise this so much (as the Rabbis do), that we feel we cannot evangelise them in a normal way. Because of this some Christians stress that we must first approach them with love, by which they mean practical expressions of love which will give emotional comfort and practical assistance. This is frequently backed up by quotations from Isaiah 40v1 with its command to 'comfort' Jews because of the afflictions they have suffered.

This is an understandable over-reaction, but it is not an approach you will find in the Scriptures. The Jews were not exactly popular in the Roman world when the (Jewish) Apostles went out with the Gospel. But we do not see men like Paul trying to prepare a way into Gentile hearts with 'love'. Furthermore, if you examine Isaiah 40 you will find that the message of comfort is the coming of God to His people, and the need for them to prepare the way for Him by humbling themselves. God's comfort is the Gospel.

The great danger of this emphasis on the need for practical expressions of love to come first is that it could appear insincere to Jewish people; just a carrot to prepare the way for the Gospel. A leading article in the 'Jewish Chronicle' of 24 April 1987 shows that this is how they do see it, and that they do not want it. It was addressed to Christian friends of Israel and included these words, 'If you offer that hand (of friendship) with respect for his beliefs and set aside all thought of seducing him to yours, it will be grasped firmly and in good fellowship. But if you have in your heart what you believe to be a 'higher purpose'...then, in sorrow but unwaveringly, we will walk separately from you.' If such love is a carrot, then that is a fair response. It has an air of deception about it, and so it is not wanted. If it is not meant as a carrot, we must still be aware that that is the way it is often seen.

There is another danger here. Does not this stress on the need for 'love' imply that the act of presenting the Gospel does not involve love, or at least not so greatly? But it is love which spurs us to preach the Gospel. It is not possible to evangelise properly without the energy of love. And from my experience I would say you will not last long in witnessing to Jews without it. It is the height of love to someone to tell them of Jesus, especially if you anticipate that you will not get much thanks for it. Surely He is the best we have to give; it is therefore a lack of love to withold Him in any way.

However, I do understand why people react to Jewish sufferings in this way. The burden of Christendom's treatment of the Jews is a very difficult one to bear in Jewish witness. But we cannot hold back the Gospel because of it. That would be disobedience to our Lord. Let me make it plain that I am not discouraging the showing of practical expressions of love to the Jews, or the giving of support to Israel's concerns. I would encourage those things; because they are your neighbour, and because they are Abraham's offspring. But let it spring out of a disinterested Christian love, and be coupled with a clear presentation of the Gospel as opportunity arises.

Earning the Right
There is another form to this over-reaction to Jewish sufferings within Christendom. It is one which says you have to earn the right to witness to them. I was once giving out tracts at Golders Green when an angry young man strode up to me and accused me of being 'a moral cripple'. Jewish suffering at the hands of 'Christians' was what was making him so indignant. For him, I had no right to preach anything to the Jews. Some Christians have felt bowled over by this, and look for ways to earn that right.

The response to this is to remember that our right to preach does not come from men, but from the Son of God who has given us a command to evangelise. It is not something which we can earn. We should certainly aim to defuse their prejudice by our manner, and perhaps by explaining who is a Christian and who is not. It may be that they will not want to hear and we will have to respect that. But none of these things affect our basic right to speak to them.

Knowledge
As this book has faced you with information about the Jews it would not be surprising if you reacted by thinking that unless you have a vast knowledge of Judaism, Jewish history, and Jewish ways you cannot begin to speak of Jesus to a Jewish friend. That is a mistake. Knowledge helps, and that is why this book has been written, but do not be intimidated into thinking that you must be an expert before you can begin. If you have read your Bible through only once, then you have done more than most in the Jewish community. You will meet only a few Jews who know the Scriptures well. When it comes to Judaism, as I have already said, ask about what you do not know; Jewish people do not expect you to know much anyway.

Living Jewishly
In this section I am especially speaking to Christians of a Gentile background, although I do not think these thoughts are irrelevant for Jewish believers. The problem being faced here is that Jewish people have lost sight of the fact that the Gospel is Jewish, and so we

need to present the Gospel in a Jewish way to make this plain to them. But it is possible to go too far in this. What I am referring to is the efforts of some who are not Jews to adopt a Jewish lifestyle.

Paul's practice in this matter is our guide, and in 1 Cor.9v20 he wrote that we should become 'as a Jew to the Jews'. Those who go too far seem to be reading this as if Paul said he became a Jew to the Jews. But they forget the little word 'as', which points to something quite different. What he means is that he temporarily adopts something of their lifestyle and culture so as get alongside them with the Gospel. It does not mean he permanently adopted that lifestyle. How could he if one day he was a Jew to the Jews and the next he was without law to those without law? To temporarily become like someone is quite different to adopting their way of life. When the Gentile Christians of Galatia began to act as if they were Jews, Paul had some strong things to say to them.

The kind of thing I am referring to today is the temptation for some to adopt Jewish customs, and perhaps to go to gatherings where Jewish believers adopt such customs. Jewish responses to this will vary. Some will see such Gentiles as odd. Others will think they are 'using' Jewish traditions. Still others will be angry or feel insulted. For most Jews such things, if they are practised at all, are for Jews only. Whilst it will be wise to occasionally adopt a Jewish practice with the aim of being sensitive to a friend, we must recognise that such things are not the Jewishness of the Gospel. The Gospel is Jewish because God has revealed Himself through the Jewish people in the Jewish Scriptures, and pre-eminently in His own coming as the Messiah promised to the Jews. Conveying those things to a Jewish friend is the way to show him that the Gospel is Jewish.

The application of this to Jewish believers is different for the simple reason that Jewish culture is their culture. This is too big a subject to go into here, but I would like to make a few remarks from what I have said above. If Paul only became as a Jew then no Jewish believer today should think it is essential to be an observant Jew if he is to win his Jewish friends to the Messiah. In fact, it may obscure the Gospel, because the unsaved Jew will assume that such Jewish believers are observant for the same reasons as orthodox Jews are - that is, to earn their salvation. Paul's way was quite different. On his own testimony he lived as unbound by Jewish traditions, and he founded churches composed of Jews and Gentiles. None of this would have endeared him to his people. But he would not allow his desire to be sensitive to his own people to undermine the fact that the New Covenant had come.

'So Much Depends On Me!'

My final point is a general one, but with all my stress on the need for understanding and sensitivity I think it should be made. If we lose sight of the fact that man cannot and will not move a millimetre towards God except by God's gracious power, then we will put too much stress on the part we have to play in evangelism. We will start to rely upon techniques to pressurise people, or become entertaining to attract them. Jesus did neither of these things. He presented the truth in the power of the Spirit, out of a godly character, and God drew sinners to Himself. And that is what we must do too. Any tendency to treat Jews as cannon-fodder for the Gospel, failing to treat them as intelligent individuals with significance in God's sight will be sure to further alienate them. Thank God that He can overrule our failures, but we must not presume He will do so.

It will help you to get your approach right if you remember that the Gospel message is to affect every part of their being; the mind, the heart (or emotions), and the will. This is clear from Paul's words to the Christians in Rome, 'you obeyed (will) from the heart (emotions) that form of doctrine (mind) to which you were delivered' (Rom. 6v17). They heard the truth and understood it, and they were moved by it so that they obeyed it. Likewise we present the truth, and in such a way that it is movingly understood, and we urge our Jewish friend to submit to it.

Yet as we do this we must be aware that it is essential that God is secretly at work, opening the eyes of their understanding, moving their hearts, and giving them a willingness to believe. This is the work of the Spirit in giving spiritual enlightenment and the new birth. Without this all will be in vain.

We present the Gospel, and trust and pray that God will do these things for them as we do so. If it does not appear that He is then we should not get frantic and start to act in an insensitive and pressurising manner, trying to do what He alone can do. We are especially prone to this temptation when presenting Messianic prophecy to Jewish people. It seems so obvious to us, why do they not believe it! Yes, it is very clear, God has made it plain; but unless they are born again then their will simply does not submit to it, even though their intellect can see it. Be patient. Reason, but do not argue; and above all pray.

19.
Some detailed advice

Your General Attitude

The last word of the previous chapter was 'pray', and that is where our personal witness begins. If we are praying for particular individuals, or for opportunities to come our way, then we will be ready and in a proper frame of mind when they do.

This book began by stressing the importance of our daily Christian life, and I want to underline that. You are already witnessing for Christ by the way you live for Him among others. Do not underestimate the usefulness of that witness, either to underline or to undermine the truthfulness of what you say. This is especially significant with Jewish people, because so much of what goes by the name of Christianity has only undermined its truthfulness to them.

Jesus Himself is the great soul-winner. It was He who first came to seek and save the lost, and He is still doing that today. He has been speaking to Jewish people whom you will meet, and through you He has more to say. If you are conscious of being a co-worker with Him, then you will experience a confidence as you witness which prevents either hesitancy or haste.

It is worth asking yourself who is to be glorified by your witness. You? Your Jewish friend? Perhaps the Jewish people? I am sure you are thinking, 'None of these, God is to be glorified!' Well just make sure that He is! We all like to talk of our experiences and of the issues of life, and when we mention God in it all, well, we often seem to view Him as just our helper. But He is our Maker and Redeemer!

The Gospel brings Him glory. If this is in our mind's eye then we will keep things in perspective.

What does your witness aim at? Many Jewish people admire Jesus as a teacher, prophet, or sage; but Jesus demands more than admiration, He requires allegiance. He is the Lord of glory, the Word made flesh, and we must bring Jewish people to Him in repentance and faith. With this in mind we will be preserved from accepting people's faint praise of Jesus as a suffcent response.

All this has certain practical consequences. To begin with you should be straightforward in what you say. Be gracious of course, but do not be mealy-mouthed. As well as this remember you are not out to defeat people in an argument, but to witness of Jesus as Messiah and Saviour; so do not be argumentative, Jesus never was. Furthermore, it does not all depend on you, so if you cannot answer a question, say so, and offer to look for the answer. That will give you an opportunity for further conversation. Make sure you do not always end up on the defensive; always dealing with your friend's questions or objections. His own wrong thinking needs to be challenged, and you are to present Christ. So answer his questions, but ensure you go on to ask your own, and to present the Saviour. I have suggested some in Appendix 4. Finally do not give up at the first rebuff. That reaction may be purely cultural. If the Lord has brought you into contact with someone no doubt He has something to say to them, so wait on Him for another opportunity.

The Witnessing Situation

I want to stress the importance of flexibility first of all. Our age demands instant solutions and frequently proposes mechanical ways to arrive at them. The church has caught this fever, and therefore modern evangelistic methods are frequently far too rigid. A technique of a set form of words is often proposed, and the impression is given that all can use it with success. How different from Jesus! Think of all His encounters with individuals in the Gospels; are there any two the same? He was so flexible in His approach, while always being determined to point people to Himself as Saviour.

The situations in which we witness can be divided into two basic groups, long term ones and short term ones, and this difference demands a flexibility in our approach. Long term situations are when we are meeting a Jewish friend day-to-day, and although we need to beware of becoming casual, yet we can afford to take our time in building up our testimony to God's truth. We do not have to say everything at once, and we may well put up barriers if we try to. As life goes on there will be all sorts of opportunities to show the Gospel by what we say and do. We should simply be ready to take them when they come.

In short term situations such as encounters in business, in travel, or at the shops, some aspect of conversation may involve a moral or spiritual principle. This is a natural opportunity to speak and we should be ready to take it. If it is rebuffed we should not insensitively press on, nor should we go on if our hearer is only politely listening. But if what we say is taken up then we should continue the conversation. The difference with the short term situation is that we do want to ensure, as far as we can, that the essentials of the Gospel are communicated. It is amazing how much can be put in one short sentence!

For example, Jewish people are just as prone as others to express shock or sorrow at disasters reported in the news. If they have not already asked it themselves, it may be suitable to ask 'Do you think there is any purpose in such things?' They will probably have no concrete answer, and it may give you the opportunity to say something like, 'I think they warn us to be ready.' You will need to explain that by being ready you do not mean avoiding planes and trains that might crash, but rather being ready to die and meet God. So you might say something like 'We all need to be ready to meet God. We have all failed to keep our own standards, let alone God's, and a day is coming when He will judge us. What the Scriptures say is that Jesus the Messiah has paid the price of sin. I have trusted in Him, and I know God has forgiven me.' With such a reply you stick to the theme, deal with fears which are common to all, and testify to the historical facts of salvation, which are relevant for all now, and which have changed you.

Are they Jewish? So far I have taken it for granted that you know your friend is Jewish, and that he knows that you know. However that is not always so, and that leads to a different witnessing situation requiring another approach. Imagine you are speaking of the Gospel to someone, but you do not know that they are Jewish. Quite early on in the conversation, perhaps as their first response, they are likely to say, 'Oh, I'm Jewish', implying that what you are saying may be very interesting but it is not for them. How do you respond? It will not be very wise to say 'Oh, that doesn't matter', and press on regardless, as if being Jewish is of no consequence, or even a disadvantage. You should take the opportunity to express a genuine appreciation of this fact. You should say that you are pleased to meet someone Jewish; and you might go on to express the gratitude you feel to his people, because through them the Scriptures, which you read daily, came to the world. You may then be able to go on to assure them that what you believe is a very Jewish message, found in the Jewish Scriptures, and that he of all people should believe it as it is part and parcel of his own history. The general point is that you must turn this discovery of their Jewishness from their view of it as a negative point, into a very positive one with respect to the Gospel.

There may be occasions when you know your friend is Jewish, or you suspect he is, but you are not certain that he knows that you are aware of this. It is important to clarify this matter before presenting the Gospel in a Jewish way. Be careful about bluntly asking 'Are you Jewish?' He may have been asked that before, but with a hostile intent. Something about him may hint at it and give you the opportunity to say something like, 'Do you mind if I ask you if you are Jewish?' A young man I once witnessed to about Jesus gave me no hint that he was Jewish but then he asked me, 'What has all you are saying got to do with the Old Testament?' To my mind only a Jew would ask such a question and so I asked him if he was Jewish. Of course, if your friend is wearing something like a skull cap (a kippa) which declares that he is Jewish, then you can easily say 'I see that you are Jewish.' With ladies a necklace with Hebrew lettering may give you a similar opportunity. As long as they do not deny it you can then continue with your presentation of the Gospel, but in a Jewish way.

All this is part of flexibility to people, but such flexibility has other consequences too. You must be prepared to listen so as to understand your friend's thoughts and feelings. I have already made it plain that Jewish people vary a great deal so ask some questions to find out more. In fact your ignorance of your Jewish acquaintance and of Judaism can be a good way to start a conversation. You might say something like, 'As someone Jewish, what do you think of this?' Or, 'What does Judaism have to say about...?' Most Jewish people will readily answer such questions, although you need to be aware that other Jews may not agree with the answer! Religious festivals give an opportunity to ask 'What do your family do at Passover?' This will probably create an opportunity to speak of Jesus as the true Passover lamb, the lamb of God. Make sure that any questions you ask are not forced, but spring from a genuine interest in their answer.

Always make sure your friend has finished what he is saying before you answer, and never interrupt. In your reply to his points always make sure you do answer them, but if you can finish with a question of your own then do so. This gives you the opportunity to keep the conversation going, and also to take the initiative with the aim of keeping things focused on what is important. Most conversations you have will not end up with your friend indicating that he is convinced and wants to trust in Jesus, although that is what you are hoping for eventually. This means that it is wise to try and leave the conversation open-ended, by which I mean finishing with a remark like 'I look forward to us being able to talk again about all this.' This leaves things on a friendly note; the idea of anyone having won a debate is absent, and so the door is left open.

A word about using the Bible. Before you take out your Bible to support a point you are making, make sure your friend is happy about you doing it. Do not assume he knows anything about the passage you have in mind so make the context plain, and having read it, explain its relevance to the point you are trying to make. In other words do not use Bible quotes like shots from a gun, but reason from them. Remember that he may not see the Bible as authoritative, but if he is prepared to listen then it is likely he has a respect for it.

Jewish people do not usually speak of 'the Bible', the term we use to describe the Old and New Testaments together. To describe the Old Testament some will speak of 'the Scriptures' or 'the Hebrew Scriptures', and others may use the more Jewish term, 'the Tanakh'. You will also hear the term 'Torah', which is usually used to describe the whole body of authoritative Jewish teachings, but also has the more narrow meaning of the the five books of Moses. When you quote from the Old Testament it is best to refer to it as 'the Hebrew Scriptures' as this conveys precisely what you mean, and refer to the New Testament either as 'the New Testament' or 'the New Testament part of the Bible'.

If you have the opportunity to sit down and present the Gospel from the Bible then begin with the Old Testament, using some of the passages mentioned earlier. Do not be afraid to quote from the New Testament, and use it to clearly show the promises of salvation fulfilled in Messiah Jesus. Not many Jewish people have a copy of the New Testament so if it is suitable you can offer to obtain one for them, or even a whole Bible if they do not have the Hebrew Scriptures either.

It may be wise to suggest reading from their translation of the Scriptures if they have one. (N.B. Few Jews can read and translate Hebrew themselves; if they read the Bible at all they use a translation of some sort.) However you should be prepared for some differences; such as the order of the Old Testament books, the numbering of the verses on a few occasions, and that the translation of certain key passages has sometimes been distorted or varied to avoid giving any support to the Christian interpretation. If you come across such a difference it is best to go to another passage which teaches the same thing, and perhaps do some homework on the reasons for the difference you encountered. It may be an opportunity for further discussion.

This leads on to another consideration: should you ever oppose the teachings of the Rabbis? Some say no to this, to avoid antagonism, but as Jesus did then I believe that there will be occasions when we will need to. Those occasions will not be when we first witness to a Jewish friend, but as his interest grows then the conflict between Jesus and the Rabbis is bound to surface. In Mark 7v1-23 we have an example of how the Lord turned opposition to His teaching, an opposition which you are bound to experience, into an exposure of how their own beliefs were obscuring the real issues. Then He used that to lead on to a clear statement of the real nature of man's problem. People's understanding of the truth is often sharpened by their wrong thinking being exposed. As long as this is done in a gracious manner, with the intent of winning them and not the argument, we should feel free to do it.

What about using your own testimony? If you are not Jewish you might be tempted to think that this will not cut much ice. That is just not true. Your testimony of what God has done for you in forgiveness, a new life, a knowledge of God, and God with you in all the ups and downs of life, is highly relevant to your Jewish friend. Feel free to speak in a natural manner of all that the God of Israel is to you. Of course the testimony of a Jewish believer does have an added dimension, and it is important to let your friend know that there are many Jews who believe in Jesus. If you know any then you can suggest introducing them to him. Most Jewish people who begin to seriously seek feel very much alone, and they imagine they are the first to think this way. Well, they are not! And it is good to let them know it. If there are no Jewish believers near to you then there are written testimonies available, either from your local Christian bookshop, or from 'Christian Witness to Israel'.

Can you invite a Jewish friend to your home? Why not? Admittedly some of the very orthodox Jews would refuse, but they are few and far between. The majority would not have any great problems about coming, especially if they are already concerned to talk further. An invitation for coffee or a meal is quite in order although it would be wise to enquire if there is anything they would not want to be offered. We often underestimate the value of our homes as a hospitable environment for witness. If you have one you should use it.

What about inviting a Jewish friend to your church? You should not assume that this is completely out of order for all Jews. It will be worth asking him when you feel his interest has developed sufficiently. Coming to a gathering of the church is more important than is often thought today. God is present in a unique way in the gatherings of His people, and this will have an effect upon unbelievers. I know of an Israeli family who were deeply impressed when they attended what we would describe as a traditional nonconformist service on the Lord's Day. They were moved by the sense of reverence coupled with freedom in all that was done. It was quite different from the average Synagogue. They were also impressed by the straightforward preaching of the Word. It is the latter which should be our main concern in inviting a Jewish friend. Preaching has always been God's prime means of bringing souls to Himself, and so if at all possible we should aim to get our Jewish friend to come and hear God's Word proclaimed.

You should be thoughtful about what type of meeting to bring him to, but do not assume it has to be a special evangelistic meeting. The example above demonstrates the value of a Lord's Day service, but a more informal home meeting may be easier for him to begin with. Whatever seems best, you should only bring your friend to a meeting which you know will be conducted in a way which is sensitive to unbelievers being present. This will ensure he does not feel out of place. It is not essential, but it may be wise, to inform whoever is leading the meeting that you are hoping to bring an unconverted Jewish friend with you.

It is usually unwise to introduce your friend to others at a church meeting as someone who is Jewish; he will probably be feeling like a fish out of water already and it will not help if you draw attention to this. You may experience problems with those who will want to buttonhole him, especially those who are in some way obsessed with the Jews. Be ready for such if you know of them, and if they do get involved and you feel it is counter-productive, then rescue your friend with something like, 'Excuse me, but I did want David to meet.....', and then take him on! It might be helpful for you to give a brief description of the meeting before you go, and if there will be an offering taken up then you should let him know that he is not expected to contribute.

Finally, a word about using literature. There is plenty of literature available which has been especially prepared for Jews. 'Christian Witness to Israel', or other agencies, can supply you with some, or your local bookshop may have some copies. It will be worth obtaining some and having it ready. If a particular topic has arisen in a conversation then you might offer some related literature with the words, 'This puts it a lot better than I can, would you like to read it? It will be a reminder of what we have been discussing.' If you offer a book it is perhaps best to lend it. This ensures it is read, and gives you an opportunity to start a discussion about it at a later time.

Written testimonies of Jewish Christians can be useful if you do not know any personally. Some of these are in booklets containing several accounts, and if one is about a Rabbi or a famous Jew it can be especially useful to counter the charge that only ignorant or insignificant members of their community get converted. However we should beware of putting too much stress on the importance of such people, remembering that Jesus rejoiced that His Father had revealed the truth to 'babes' rather than the 'wise and prudent'. We should not be surprised if that is so today, nor should we be ashamed of it.

Let me finish this chapter where it began, on the note of prayer. As you begin to speak with a Jewish friend about Jesus be in a prayerful frame of mind as the discussion develops. You need guidance and wisdom, and you need to speak with grace and authority. Only God can supply you with these.

20.
Leading to Messiah, and to His people

It is a thrilling experience to see someone to whom you have been witnessing becoming more and more open to the Lord Jesus. They have objected to one degree or another, but now they are listening more and more. A genuine repentance along with a sense of their need of salvation has developed, but as yet they have not believed. What do you do now? What part do you have to play? And when they have come to faith, what then? I want to try to answer these questions in this chapter.

Leading to Messiah

Your responsibility is to make the Gospel message plain, and to urge your Jewish friend to respond to God through Jesus the Messiah. You must make it plain to him that he is a sinner before God, and that he needs to repent. You must point him to Jesus as the promised Saviour who alone can save him from judgement. Be sure that he has counted the cost of this step. He is probably apprehensive of the consequences and you must not try to diminish these. But you should assure him that the Lord's grace is suffcient. You should reason with him and urge him to believe the Gospel. That involves three things: he must confess his sin; he must trust Messiah Jesus for forgiveness and thank Him for dying for sinners; and he must receive Jesus as Saviour and Lord.

It is not your responsibility to be present when he comes to God in this way. He may want you to be present, but it is not necessary;

in fact you may be a hindrance. Does this surprise you? Surely it is standard practice to be with a person and pray with them. Perhaps it is, but you will be hard put to find it specifically mentioned in the Gospels or the Acts. We do not read of the Lord Jesus, or the Apostles who followed His example, personally praying with people at conversion. They placed the truth before men, urged them to believe it, and then let them have personal dealings with God. Look at how Philip dealt with the Ethiopian (Acts 8v35,36), or how Paul handled those who responded to his preaching in Antioch (Acts 13v43). In both cases, once the message was preached and urged, the personal initiative to come to God was taken by the sinner, not the messenger. This is a good example to follow, and I would suggest several reasons for it.

There is always the danger that if we pray with someone then we will get in the way. The work of the Spirit and the thoughts of a person's heart are not known to us, so we should be very cautious of assuming we know what is happening. God is very varied in His dealings with men, and so we should be careful of getting too involved in the final stages. The danger is that we will produce Christians whose conversion is very similar to our own.

Coming to Jesus for salvation is a very personal thing. It is a spiritual union; and like the marriage union, it is intimate. I would not press this too far, but there may be sins to be confessed, or anguish or joy to be expressed, which are for Christ's ears only. In such circumstances your presence will be inhibiting, and could encourage a shallow first encounter with the Saviour. There is also the danger of our pride. Sometimes our reason for being there is to stake our claim. Any such attitude will have a quenching effect.

All this means that I would also resist the idea of presenting your friend with a set prayer to pray. We do not see such a practice in the New Testament, and it runs the risk of limiting the freedom of the Spirit. Unless your friend asks you to pray with him then I would suggest that you simply urge him to get alone with God and pour out his heart to Him. Later on you can ask him if he has done so, and then take things from there.

Some advice for the early days

In all normal circumstances the New Testament has no concept of Christian growth apart from the church. It is in that context that believers are taught, have fellowship with God and with one another, and pray together(Acts 2v42). This may present special difficulties for Jewish Christians, but it is the goal to aim for.

The difficulties may be due to all the problems of the past, or the problem of letting the family know. Whatever it may be, be patient. Give your friend all the support you can through one-to-one Bible study and prayer together. Lend him good books and sermons on cassette. Introduce him to other Christians from your church, and to Jewish Christians if possible. If you have church gatherings off the church premises, that may be an easier start for him.

In the last chapter I made some comments on bringing a Jewish friend to church. Most of those still apply now that your friend is a believer, whether he finds it difficult to come or not. If a deep work has been done in his heart then despite his reservations, he will be looking forward to meeting other Christians and growing with them. Even when he has started to come to church it will be important to spend time with him in Bible study and prayer, but as time goes on, and he begins to receive strength from other members of the body, then the need for such one-to-one help should fade away.

On a personal level you should encourage him in his own reading of the Bible and in prayer. Give him some guidance on the various study aids which can help him with this. As well as this, encourage him to tell others of his faith, although this should not be necessary if he is knowing anything of the power of the Spirit upon him!

What of witnessing to his family and other Jewish people? This does need particular sensitivity, and it is difficult to make rules because each situation and the personalities involved are so different. However, with all the sensitivity and wisdom in the world it is impossible to avoid the profound shock that this will be to his family and friends. But if the blow can be softened then it may reduce whatever difficulties will be experienced in the future. It may also help them to be open to Jesus the Messiah. Encourage your friend to talk about it with you, with your Pastor, and with a mature Jewish believer. He should not speak or act hastily without thought or prayer. Young believers can be too blunt in telling others of their faith, and in a way that lacks sensitivity to the thinking of their hearers. Do not misunderstand me. I would not want these remarks to quench a bold and joyful sharing of Jesus, but simply to encourage a sensitivity to the one being spoken to.

It is very likely that his Jewish friends and family have already observed his interest in religion and the Scriptures. It may have led to some personal discussion with them on such matters. Once he is converted, such a time of discussion will be an ideal opportunity to speak of his new faith. It may even arise out of them asking him questions. Hopefully they will have noticed a change in him, and that may lead to questions being asked. It will probably be best to wait for a while before saying anything, just to see if such a natural opportunity arises. But it may not, or circumstances may prevent it; well, he cannot wait forever. He will have to take the initiative himself, and he will have to look to the Lord to make the way plain.

Whatever the circumstances, one thing is central to the manner in which he speaks of his new faith: he must present his faith in Jesus as the fulfilment of his Jewish heritage. He has come back to the God of Israel through the Messiah promised in the Scriptures. His sins are forgiven, he has come to know God, and he has a new love for His law. What could be more Jewish! This was what God formed Israel for. It will therefore be wise for him to avoid expressions which reinforce the Jewish assumption that a believer in Jesus is no longer a Jew. 'I have found the Messiah' (see John 1v41), will therefore be better than 'I have become a Christian.' Of course, wise terminology can never completely remove the tension. He will also need to beware of being so Jewish in his presentation that he ends up appearing to deny the universal nature of the Gospel, or that the Covenant he has come into is God's new one. Nevertheless, with a little wisdom he can help his family and friends to see that he has not changed to a Gentile religion, but has gone back to his Biblical Jewish roots as they are fulfilled in Jesus. That is surely what he wants for them too.

However, they may not want it. And they may want him to see some sense and come back to the fold. Pressure may come in many forms. They may insist he sees a Rabbi or goes on a Jewish summer camp. How to respond to this pressure will vary greatly according to circumstances, but the church must surround him with its love and support. The conflict between the Jewish leaders and the man born blind (John 9v17-34) shows how the Lord can help the weakest to confound the mighty. The Lord Jesus can keep those He saves. This should prevent us from getting into too much of a panic as we try to help. However, in that account Jesus soon 'found him'; the church cannot just leave the young convert to it, but must pray for him and help him to deal with the arguments.

What about water Baptism? Jewish family and friends will see this as the point of no return. As long as this has not taken place they may still attempt to win him back, or somehow explain away all his interest in Christianity in the hope that it will not last. But any talk of baptism will cause real shock waves. Because of this it will be tempting to view it as optional; but it is not. Jesus has commanded it. Furthermore it is not to be secret, because its whole purpose is to be a public profession of faith. There may be good reasons for delaying it, as long as that does not become an excuse for avoiding its costliness. This is not a problem which only Jews face, and it may be useful to remind your friend of this. As he makes known his intention to be baptised, and as the time approaches, he should be given plenty of support in fellowship and prayer. It is unusual these days for someone to be ejected from his family, but it does happen and baptism may trigger this. In his sorrow, grief and loss, he will be upheld by his experience of the love of Christ and the love of his local church.

Being a Jewish Christian

Accepted Jewish thinking on Jesus means that unsaved Jews cannot square the idea of being a Jew and a Christian. But that is not so for Jewish Christians! For them nothing could be more compatible, despite the difficult questions it raises. For most of them, coming to faith gives them their first understanding of what being Jewish is all about.

Unfortunately for the Jewish Christian it may not only be his Jewish friends who are in difficulties over this. There are Christians who may say to him 'Of course, you're not a Jew any longer; you've become a Christian.' He is surrounded by people who think he is no longer Jewish! But of course such people would not say this sort of thing about an Indian Hindu. They may not be Hindu any longer, but they are still Indian, and would be expected to live according to many Indian ways. But why cannot a Jewish Christian be viewed in the same way? Surely he should be.

Why is there this confusion? It is because a wrong conclusion is being drawn from a well-known truth. It is true that the Mosaic

Covenant that God made with Israel has been replaced by the New Covenant made with all those who have faith in Jesus the Messiah (Jer. 31v31-34; Heb. 8v7-13). But it is wrong to conclude from this that a Jew who enters the New Covenant is no longer Jewish. Try telling that to Peter or Paul! If anyone is born Jewish they remain Jewish. Many Christians have this picture in their minds that by definition a Jew is someone who keeps the law of Moses and a multitude of Rabbinic customs. That is how the Rabbis want us all to think. So when a Jew believes in Jesus many Christians assume that, as he will no longer do such things, then he is no longer Jewish. But that is not what makes someone Jewish. Rather, it is descent from Abraham, Isaac, and Jacob; and those Patriarchs did not know much about the Law of Moses and the traditions of the Rabbis! Jewish Christians are still very Jewish, but they will not express it according to the Rabbinic definition, if they ever did in the first place. So, how will that Jewishness be expressed? That is the question your friend will need some help with.

Some might be tempted to ask, 'Is it important?' Well, it is good for any of us to be clear about who we are! It is good to be able to express and enjoy the valuable things of the culture in which we were raised. As well as that it is obviously important for your friend's testimony to his fellow Jews. He wants them to see that he has not deserted his people in becoming a believer in Jesus. It is also important as a permanent testimony to the world that Jew and Gentile can be united in Jesus the Messiah.

I believe that this is too large a subject to be dealt with fully in this book, but I think it is possible to suggest some guidelines. As I have already mentioned, for one born a Jew the most important expression of Jewishness is to believe in the God of Israel, to love the Jewish Scriptures and to trust in Jesus the Messiah promised to the Jews. Such a faith in its Old Testament form marked out Abraham, and without it the other aspects of Jewishness are worthless. Jews who are critical of a Jewish Christian need to be reminded of that first and foremost. So too do Christians who have forgotten that Christianity is Jewish.

But there is more to being Jewish than that; there is the cultural aspect of Jewishness. We are all born into a certain culture, and each culture is influenced by religion, the events of its history, the climate, the available food, etc.etc. Your culture is one; the American, the Egyptian, the Chinese, the Brazilian, the Angolan, are others. The Jewish culture is another. Now when anyone becomes a Christian in any of these cultures there will be a clash at some points. For instance most cultures have a dominant religion or philosophy which requires participation in certain events. Not to participate is to appear disloyal. For the early Christians it was offering incense to the Roman Emperor; but they would not, and so there was a clash. For Jews today it might be participation in the Rabbinic stipulations for the Day of Atonement. But those are a denial of the Biblical way of salvation, and so they cannot do it. However, certain aspects of culture are matters of indifference, food being a simple example. Like other Christians a Jew who believes in Jesus will retain many aspects of his culture which do not cause a clash, and they will be a further expression of his Jewishness. Bearing in mind that for many unsaved Jews these things are the most important part of Jewishness, it becomes clear how important this is.

It is all too easy for Christians, particularly those in the Western cultures where many Jews live, to assume that their culture is 'Christian', and so they expect Jewish Christians to be like them at almost every point. But such Christians would benefit from taking a detached look at their own lifestyle and asking themselves how much of it is clearly commanded in the New Testament, how much of it is their application of Biblical principles, and how much of it is a matter of indifference as far as Scripture is concerned. If we are going to help Jewish Christians in these matters we need to have a clear view of our own lifestyle. For example, in the area of 'Christian' festivals, such as Easter, Jewish Christians may have real difficulties with being involved. Must they be? Are such festivals stipulated in the New Covenant?

Let me suggest a few more practical thoughts. If someone Jewish has been brought up to enjoy eating bagels and gefilte fish, does he have to start eating only the same things as the majority of Christians around him? Does he have to start eating pork if he never did before? And then what about history? A Jewish Christian can look back on certain events with great joy; events such as the Exodus, or the deliverance from Haman. Is he not entitled to remember them, to celebrate them, in some way? For centuries there have been traditional ways of doing this in Jewish homes, and these can be used and adapted. Of course there is need for care over any elements which are unbiblical or even anti-Biblical. For instance, remembering the

events of Purim is good, but the tradition of having too much to drink
is not! There is also the need to heed the warning in Hebrews 13v9
against the danger of getting preoccupied with such matters; it is
Christ who is to preoccupy us. However, the events themselves are
surely something to rejoice in. What I am suggesting here is not to
go back under the law because there is no compulsion about it. In
fact not all of the things commemorated would be events of the
Biblical period. But surely it is natural for Jewish believers to
remember the enjoyable things — and the unpleasant things — of
their people's past. Things which are often more worthwhile remembering than the events commemorated in many Gentile cultures!

As well as all this a Jewish Christian can express his Jewishness
by maintaining his involvement in the Jewish community. This may
be made difficult for him, but not always. A Jewish believer I know
works in a Jewish Day Centre. It may also mean participating in
Jewish concerns for Israel; in fact that is probably one of the easiest
ways of remaining involved. And then, of course, as he maintains
contact with his family his Jewishness will continue to be expressed.
These suggestions are not exhaustive, a lot more could be said, but
I think they cover the main areas.

I hope it is understood that the context in which I am making
these remarks about Jewishness is the one of your friend's home, his
family and friends. I am not suggesting that a local church, in
whatever culture it is set, should imagine that it has a free hand in
deciding what traditions it will develop. When Paul wrote 'Therefore, brethren, stand fast and hold the traditions which you were
taught, whether by word or our epistle' (2 Thess. 2v15), he makes it
plain that there were traditions to be kept, such as the basic form of
the Lord's Supper. Of course, the manner in which they are engaged
in will depend on the particular character and circumstances of that
group of believers, but the lifestyle of a local church is not something we have a free hand in. A Jewish believer can rejoice that the
most important traditions of the local church are derived from his
people's Biblical heritage; by which I mean the Scriptures of the Old
and New Testaments, the preaching of God's Word, the Lord's
Supper based on the Passover, baptism based on a Jewish ritual for
proselytes, and an Eldership modelled on Israel's leadership pattern.

In saying this I do not want to appear dismissive of the sincerity or service of those Jewish Christians who believe it is right to form Messianic Congregations. These are local churches which have Jewish traditions as part of their worship and their annual festivals. They are frequently justified by the desire to create an environment which unsaved Jewish visitors will not find alien, and by the desire on the part of Jewish believers to express their Jewishness. I very much sympathise with such desires, but I believe they can and should be fulfilled outside the formal gatherings of the local church, often in a more private context.

My reason for saying this is that, as I have written above, we do not have a free hand to bring into the local church any traditions we want. Paul did not introduce such Jewish traditions into the churches he founded, which were composed of Jews and Gentiles, and so we are not at liberty to do so. His reason for not doing so is surely clear. Christ has broken down the middle-wall of partition between Jew and Gentile, which consisted of the regulations of the Mosaic Covenant (Ephesians 2v14,15). Those laws kept them apart, and to re-introduce them to the worship of God's people is to re-erect the wall. The life and traditions of the church are to exhibit the glory of being 'one new man' in the Lord Jesus. Our individual and national character differences will produce diversity and colour in that unity, but any expression of that diversity in specific ceremonies belongs to the realm of the home, family and friends.

Christians from a Gentile background, especially a Western one, should take this to heart. How much of their own familiar church ritual can be justified from the New Testament? Additions to what the New Testament requires can act as a 'middle-wall' to Jewish Christians, often making it more difficult for a new Jewish believer to discern the essential Jewishness of the New Testament Church. We expect Jewish Christians to adapt to a New Testament Church lifestyle; are we prepared to?

I hope all this has not put you off witnessing to Jewish people! Some of these matters do need thought and careful handling, but the joy of seeing people saved and growing in their love to God makes it all worthwhile.

21.
A final word

I hope that after reading the last 125 pages you feel you know a little more, and can be more sensitive to your Jewish friend. Good! But I am sure you do not need me to remind you that only the Lord Himself can save anyone; so remember to PRAY. Because of all the difficulties, do remember to be PATIENT. Then, have CONFIDENCE IN GOD'S WORD, because He is wanting to speak to Jewish people and draw them to Himself.

The Lord bless you, and don't forget that of all the Jewish people who trust in Jesus the Messiah, the majority of them gained their first interest through the testimony of a Christian friend; someone like you. So speak up! Don't let down your Lord — or your Jewish friend!

Appendix 1
Some significant dates

(N.B. c = 'about')

BC	c2000	Life of Abraham
	c1280	Exodus from Egypt
	1010-970	Reign of David
	587	Jerusalem falls to Babylonians; final deportations
	537	Rebuilding of the Temple
	c470	Haman attempts to destroy the Jews
	c430	Last of the Prophets; Malachi
	169	Antiochus Epiphanes desecrates the Temple
	165	Rededication of Temple by the Maccabees
	63	Roman conquest of Jerusalem
AD	c28-30	Public ministry of Jesus the Messiah
	c30	Apostles begin preaching in Jerusalem
	c33	Conversion of Paul
	47-57	Paul's missionary journeys
	66-73	First Jewish war with Rome
AD	70	Capture of Jerusalem; Temple destroyed
	c200	Publication of the Mishna
	312	Rome's patronage of the Church commences
	c500	Completion of the Babylonian Talmud
	c637	Arab conquest of Palestine
	1099-129	Palestine conquered by the Crusaders
	1290,1394	The Jews expelled from England,and France

1480	Spanish Inquisition set up
1492	The Jews expelled from Spain
1654	First settlement of Jews in North America
1655	Cromwell favours Jews coming to England
1730	Chasidic movement in Eastern Europe
1787,1791,1858	Full civil liberties for Jews in USA, France, England
1880	Significant resettlement of Palestine begins
1917	Balfour declaration
1941-19545	Nazi massacres of the Jews
1948	Establishment of the State of Israel
1948,1967,1973	Arab-Israeli wars
1978	Camp David Accord
1982	Israeli invasion of Lebanon

Appendix 2
Other significant prophecies

At the end of chapter 16 I have listed out the main prophecies of the Messiah, but there are other predictions of the Prophets which are important in Jewish witness. The following are some of them.

Theme	Old Testament Prediction	New Testament Fulfilment
A New Covenant will replace the Mosaic one	Jer. 31v31-34	Lk. 22v20; 2Cor. 3v6; Heb. 8v7-13
Messiah will come before the destruction of the Temple	Dan. 9v24-27	Matt. 24v15,16 Lk. 21v20-22
Messiah will send God's Word to all nations	Gen. 22v18; Isa. 11v10, Isa. 49v6	Acts 10v34-48, 19v18-20 Rom. 15v18,19
The coming of God's Spirit on all types of people	Joel 2v28,29	Acts 2v1-4,14-21, 10v44-47
The inclusion of Gentiles among God's people on an equal basis	Isa. 56v3-8; Amos 9v11,12	Eph. 2v11-22 1Pet. 2v4-10
Messiah and His people will be opposed by rulers and peoples	Psa. 2, 110v1,2; Zech. 13v7	Mk. 14v53-65; Acts 4v1-31, 16v16-40, 17v1-15

Theme	Old Testament Prediction	New Testament Fulfilment
Israel to be scattered among the Gentiles	Zech. 10v9; Ez. 39v23 (NT prediction: Lk. 21v24) destroyed	70 AD, Romans Temple & dispersed Jews
The Jews to be preserved from destruction	Jer. 31v35-37, (NT prediction: Lk. 21v24, significance of 'until')	Seen in history
The return of the Jews to the territory God gave to Abraham	Isa. 11v11,12; Joel 3v1,2 Ez. 39v25-29 (NT fulfilment: Lk. 21v24, significance of 'until')	Seen in 20th century
Jerusalem to become a focal point of world conflict	Zech. 12v2,3, 14v1,2	Awaiting fulfilment. Begun already?
A national turning of the Jews to Messiah Jesus	Zech. 12v10-13v2; Ez. 39v21-29 (NT predictions: Rom. 11v25-27; Matt. 23v38,39)	Awaiting fulfilment
The Final Judgement Day	Isa. 66v15,16; Joel 3v14-16 (NT predictions: Matt. 25v31-46; 2Thess. 1v7-10)	Awaiting fulfilment

Appendix 3
Frequent responses

These are not arranged in any particular order, except that the earlier ones are those which are more frequently expressed. The doctrinal ones are towards the end.

'I'm Jewish.'
This is a very frequent one, which I dealt with when suggesting how to respond when your friend informs you for the first time that he is Jewish. See pages 111, 112 for my suggestions.

'We Jews are alright, go to those who have no belief.'
If we judge by human standards of ethical behaviour, the Jews are frequently to be commended. However we must judge by God's Word. Isaiah was a Jew whose life was a model of piety and good behaviour, but in the presence of God he felt hopelessly sinful and unclean (Isa. 6v5). This is the situation of us all before the Holy One of Israel.

 'But how can a Jew be a Christian?'
Jews feel this is impossible because, being born Jewish, they assume Christians were born Christians. For them it is simply a matter of birth and nothing can change that. It must be explained that no-one is born a Christian. A Christian is someone who at some point in his life puts his trust in Jesus as God's appointed Saviour. Jews, as others, can and should do this. This involves a spiritual change, which all sinners need, whether Jew or Gentile. Both these concepts, faith and spiritual change, are Old Testament ones. Abraham had to

exercise personal faith in God when he left Ur, and Jesus expected
Nicodemus to be aware of the need to be born again (Jn. 3v10). That
all the first believers in Jesus were Jews is an important point here,
as is the fact that as Jesus is the Messiah, there is nothing more
Jewish than to trust in Him.

'Do you want to convert me?'
Jews think of conversion purely in terms of changing religion. They
are assuming their religion is alright, and having been born into it
they are therefore alright too. Conversion is therefore unnecessary.
But conversion in the Bible is concerned with a radical turning from
sin to God on the part of one who is a born rebel (Acts 3v19; Psalm
51v13). This is what they have to see.

Jews have an understandable emotional aversion to the term
'convert' due to past efforts to force them to change religion. What
is necessary is a change from something that cannot save to a faith
which trusts in God's way of salvation. This was seen in Abraham
when he turned to follow the LORD.

'Look at the way that Christians have treated the Jews!'
Profound sorrow must be expressed that Jews have suffered in the
name of Jesus. The 'Christians' Jews usually have in mind are those
who have justified their violent mistreatment of Jews by declaring
they were honouring Jesus and the Church. The Crusaders, the
Inquisition, and many pogromists would be in this group. They
would also have in mind those Gentiles who have expressed dislike
or hatred of the Jews and who have been brought up in countries
deeply influenced by Christianity. The Nazis would come into this
category; so, sadly, would some true Christians who have expressed
such sinful feelings.

The ones who feature most in Jewish thinking are those who
have violently mistreated the Jews, and it must be pointed out that
they could not be Christians, whatever their claims. Stalin claimed
to be a socialist, but not many socialists today would want to own
him; so too many have been called Christian whose lives deny the
possibility. It has to be admitted that some Christians have expressed wrong attitudes towards the Jews, and this is to be greatly
regretted, but such are a small number and not generally the ones
that Jews have in mind when they make this objection. It is

Christendom, usually led by unregenerate 'Christians' which they have in mind.

It is important to point out that true Christians also suffered at the hands of these false Christians. You should also draw attention to what the New Testament teaches by example and precept, that Christians are to love the Jews (e.g. Rom. 9v1-5).

It achieves nothing for a Christian to express some vague repentance over this, anymore than you would expect Jews today to repent because of what some of their leaders did to Jesus. There can only be repentance if you are personally guilty in this matter.

'Why have we suffered so much?'

Such a question may not be an attack on Christianity. Be careful not to go in at the deep end on this one; start on a human level. As one Rabbi put it, 'It is not why God allowed such things which troubles me, it is that men did them.' It says a lot about man's sinful nature. Draw attention to that.

Then it needs to be pointed out that man's sinful rebellion against God will inevitably be directed at those who are His, whether Jewish or Christian. Added to this is the malice of Satan, who seeks their destruction.

Finally there is the vexed question of God's part in it all. If God did not deliver them, but allowed such sufferings, then He must have had a reason for withdrawing His protection. It is indeed a judgement, as Moses makes clear. Orthodox Judaism would agree with such sentiments. This matter of judgement should only be mentioned with great care. It is best to suggest that they read for themselves what Moses wrote in Leviticus 26v27-39. The sin is that of not listening to God, and this found its worst expression in rejecting the words of Messiah Jesus (see Jn. 5v46,47). This in no way gives approval to man's wickedness in persecuting them. Whatever God's purposes may be, man is responsible for his actions. For instance, Peter's statement about the crucifixion of Jesus describes how God overrules man's wickedness to bring about His own set purposes, and yet man is fully responsible for his actions.(Acts 2v23).

'Not many Jews, or Jewish leaders, believe in Jesus'

The assumption that lies behind this statement is that something is more likely to be true when the majority believe it. So, if only a few

Jews follow one who says he is Messiah, it stands to reason he is not. After all, if God sends the Messiah to Israel surely they will believe.

Such an argument seems very reasonable, but it does not compare well with Israel's past dealings with God. Moses was rejected by the majority of Israel in the wilderness, and David frequently felt himself to be alone; Elijah knew of only a few believers in his day, and Isaiah spoke of a remnant. The fact is that the faithful in Israel have always been in a minority, and therefore we should not be surprised if that is so today. Isaiah spoke of Israel's unbelief concerning the Messiah when he wrote 'who has believed our report?' (Isa. 53v1).

Having said all that, there are still more Jews who believe in Jesus than is generally thought. In terms of percentage there are usually as many converted Jews per head of the Jewish population in a country, as there are converted Gentiles per head of population in that country. The heart of the problem is that so few Jews are prepared to examine the Scriptures to see what Messiah is like. A Jewish person who makes this response should be challenged as to whether he has seriously studied the Scriptures to see what he is to expect of the Messiah.

'No educated orthodox Jew would believe in Jesus'
This is a piece of Rabbinic propaganda which is totally untrue. The argument goes around in a circle because if any such Jews do believe, then it is said that they could not have been really educated or orthodox Jews, because if they were they would not believe in Jesus! However, many such Jews have believed, Saul of Tarsus and Nicodemus being two good New Testament examples. The stories of others are in print, and books such as 'Jewish Christian Leaders' contain a number of them.

'The miracles and the resurrection of Jesus cannot be taken seriously'
It does not help that 'Christian' leaders say this too! All the usual proofs for the reliability of the New Testament and the facts of the resurrection of Jesus can be used here. There are two further considerations which are relevant to Jews. The first is that they need to remember that the methods which men have adopted to cast doubt on the reliability of the New Testament Scriptures are used equally upon the Old Testament Scriptures. If they are valid for one they are

also valid for the other. For instance if someone can believe Moses led Israel through the Red Sea by a miracle, why can he not believe in the miracles of Jesus? We know of both on the simple evidence of the one who recorded it, supported by the testimony of the others present.

The second consideration follows on from this. If all these miracles did not happen, then, bearing in mind the unwelcome success of the Apostle's preaching, we would expect the Jewish leadership to have produced a collection of eyewitness testimonies that these things did not really take place. There were enough people like Saul of Tarsus to make the effort! We would also expect such evidence to have been handed down, because the controversy has never died. But the fact is that no such record exists, and that is highly significant. The reason no one made the effort is that the miracles just could not be denied by Jesus' contemporaries, and so they just hoped that the problem would go away (Acts 5v33-40).

'But how can we believe the Bible today?'

This should be answered in all the usual ways, making plain that trust in God's power to convey and preserve His Word is essential. Jews should be particularly reminded that if the Bible cannot be trusted then they have no reliable record of their own history. You should 'provoke to jealousy' by testifying how you experience God's blessings as you believe what He has said.

The remaining responses are more doctrinal in their nature.

'Why is there no world peace if Messiah has come?'

To bring peace is indeed the Messiah's work, but to think this will be done in some sort of 'Hey Presto' fashion is to ignore the passages of the Scriptures which detail how Messiah will do this. This sort of thinking is just worldliness.

The first thing to point out is that in the Scriptures peace is always connected to righteousness (see Isa. 57v21, 26v2,3). This is something which we all manifestly lack, but to experience peace with God and with one another we must have it. Clearly we need to be transformed – that is the key to this peace – but first we need to be forgiven. To make this possible Messiah Jesus suffered for sinners, so as to remove guilt (Isa. 53). Forgiveness is then received through repentance and faith in Him. By God's power, transformed, righteous lives will follow. Peace with one another is a consequence of this. To bring all this about, the world has to hear of Messiah, repent, and be transformed. Time is obviously going to be needed for all this, and who are we to say how long? It is going on now.

Then it must be pointed out that Messiah's reign is not all sweetness and light, but He will in fact experience great opposition to His rule. For instance, Psa. 110v2 speaks of many enemies who oppose the progress of His kingdom. The Lord Jesus experiences this now as He reigns from heaven, and many oppose the preaching of the Word of God. But He will succeed. The full glory of a perfect world will come one day, and Jesus spoke of that taking place when He returns. At present God is seeking the repentant people who will populate it.

Jewish people often fail to notice that there is no time scale in the Scriptures for the achievement of all these things by the Messiah; it is never said that it will all happen in a moment. In fact Isaiah can speak of a period of hundreds of years as 'a very little while' (Isa. 29v17).

'We do not need a Mediator, we can go straight to God'
Such statements are based on great ignorance of the Scriptures; an ignorance which the Rabbis have done nothing about. The Angel of the Covenant was a Mediator (Ex.23v20-21), as was Moses(Ex. 20v18-20). The whole sacrifical system made it clear to the Jews that they could not draw near to God as they were; a priest and a sacrifice were needed (Lev. 16v29-34).

'Today we do not need sacrifices; repentance is sufficent'
This is an unscriptural Rabbinic teaching. Time after time the Old Testament makes plain the need for blood sacrifice, and explains why in Lev. 17v11. It is God's ordained means of atonement to deal with the penalty which the law of Moses demands for sin. Nowhere has God set this aside, and everyone who trusts in Jesus' sacrifice is submitting to this teaching of God's Word. Repentance is indeed required of us, but we are never told that it makes an atonement for our sin.

'How can you believe that we are completely sinful?'
The Jewish belief that we are only prone to sin, coupled with the fact

that most Jews are respectable people, is what prompts this response to the teaching of the Bible that there is nothing good in us. We must explain that this does not mean that we are all as bad as we can be, or are being as evil as possible all the time. We do recognise that God's gifts to all men help us to live reasonably, and even kindly and sacrificially. What it does mean is that as a consequence of Adam's sin we are born with a nature which is sinful, so that nothing we do can please God. We cannot improve ourselves in His sight and we cannot atone for our own sins. Isa. 53v6, 64v6 and Jer. 17v9 are three Old Testament verses which teach all this. Isaiah's reaction when he saw the LORD (Isa. 6) makes these points vividly.

The wars and barbarities of this 'enlightened' century should be enough to demonstrate what we are like when we allow our outward civility to fall away. That is how God sees us all the time.

'How can you believe that Jesus became God?'

Jewish thinking about Jesus is frequently the wrong way round. It is often assumed that Christians believe that Jesus became God. It has to be made plain that He is God with us. At the bottom of such objections is a sinful human desire to limit God to what we can accept. But are we to limit God to what we think He can do? If He wishes to unite Himself with a human nature, made in His image, can He not do so? True, it is beyond us, but creatures should expect that their Creator will do things which are incomprehensible to them. He revealed to the Prophets that He would do this, and the things Jesus said and did made plain that He was indeed God with us.

'Don't Christians believe in three Gods?'

This is a further, and understandable, wrong view of Biblical teaching. It should be pointed out that Jesus stressed the oneness of God (Mk. 12v29), as did the Apostle Paul (1Cor. 8v4). But He also made it clear that there are three distinct Persons in the Godhead (Matt. 28v19). This is not inconsistent with certain Old Testament passages, such as Psa. 45v1-7, where a plurality of Persons in the one God is suggested. However, you must recognise that God did not make His Triune nature clear before Jesus came. By all means draw attention to such things, but beware of spending too much time on them. The emphasis of the New Testament is on the person of Jesus and His Divinity; the Tri-unity of God follows on from that.

'Isaiah 7v14 does not refer to a 'virgin', but to a young woman'
There are two words in Hebrew which can mean 'virgin'–
'bethulah' and 'almah'. 'Bethulah' is a more technical term and can
refer to someone of any age. 'Almah', the word in Isa. 7v14, has a
more precise meaning, similar to 'a young maiden' in older style
English. It means a young woman, who is of a marriageable age, and
is of an unblemished moral reputation. It has a special loveliness
which 'bethulah' entirely lacks. Mary fitted every aspect of this
meaning. All these aspects can be seen in each of the seven places
where it is used in the Old Testament, the meaning being determined
by the context. It does indeed describe a young woman, but always
a young woman who is a virgin. This translation is therefore best
because it highlights the supernatural element in the prediction. Its
significance is the sinlessness of the Messiah. One who is not lost
like we are, but one who can save.

'Why don't you keep the law of Moses?'
Orthodox Jewish teaching insists on the everlasting nature of the
Mosaic Covenant. The prophecy of Jer. 31v31-34 which speaks of
the Mosaic Covenant being replaced by a New Covenant is given
little significance; many Jews have never heard of it. But the fact is
that the New Covenant has now come through the Messiah and so
believers, whether Jew or Gentile, are not under the law of Moses
as a covenant code. However, it must be underlined that the law of
Moses is not ignored in the New Covenant, rather, it is vital to us
who believe. But in the New Covenant it is internalised (Jer. 31v33),
and the principles of righteousness which it teaches us are essential
to our knowledge of God's ways, and are to be obeyed (Rom. 8v4).

It might be appropriate to answer this sort of question by a
question, such as, 'Do you?' On a practical level it is impossible for
Jews today to keep the law of Moses because there is no Temple. On
a spiritual level, who has ever kept it? Their very question indicates
a failure to face up to the perfection required by the law of Moses.
Putting these two thoughts, of the practical and the spiritual,
together, it can be pointed out that God removed the Temple and the
Mosaic Covenant because its fulfilment by Jesus the Messiah on our
behalf paved the way for the life of faith; a faith which they must
have if they are to meet the law's requirements.

Appendix 4
Some Questions to ask

It is easy to be always on the receiving end of questions, especially if the person to whom you are talking is antagonistic. Make sure you ask some yourself; questions which will get to the heart of the matter. Here are some suggestions.

What do you think we are here for?
What is the point of Jewishness?
What is the point of your being Jewish?
What is your guide in life?
What do you think of the Bible?
What do you think God is like?
Why do you think the Jews have survived against such odds?
What does Judaism have to say about...?
What do you think of the Ten Commandments?
Do you believe in life after death?
Do you think we can enjoy a personal relationship with God?
How will you get your sins forgiven?
How do you explain all the evil in the world?
What do you expect the Messiah to do?
Who do you think Jesus is?
Why can't a Jew believe in Jesus?

For Further Help

This book cannot answer all the questions you may have or give detailed advice for every situation. If you want to know more or discuss a particular questions or situation, then *Christian Witness to Israel* has many staff experienced in different aspects of Jewish evangelism. Please feel free to contact us.

If you want to do some further reading or special studies then we would be happy to give advice.

Christian Witness to Israel
166 Main Road
Sundridge
Sevenoaks
Kent, TN14 6EL

Tel: 0959 565955   Fax: 0959 565966